The 4 Hour Work Week

Tool Box

The Practical Guide to Living The 4 Hour Life

George Smolinski, M.D

&

Meg Smolinski

INTRODUCTION

Tim Ferriss is my hero.

Tim, if you're reading this, your book has inspired millions including me. You have taught us a new way to live and for that, we are appreciative. But, you missed a few details, my friend.

For any of us that have read The 4 Hour Work Week, we *know* the value of instilling Tim's methods in our lives. But, there's something lacking in his book. He explains the "why", but in many instances, he leaves out the "how". That's where this book comes in to play.

In 2011, I had an enormous, life-changing event, and it made me take stock of my life. I realized I needed to change, and Tim's book fell on the fertile soil of my brain. His ideas grew and blossomed, and I've embraced his ideas and concepts in all areas of my life.

I know that many of you struggle with the "how", and that's exactly how I want to help you: I want to give you the "how" to complement the "why" in Tim's book, and those efforts are reflected in this book.

It's not complete, though, and it may never be. Technology changes rapidly, and although I'm publishing this today, in 3 years, these ideas may be obsolete. Rest assured, I'll work on publishing an updated version, but use these concepts and ideas to get started NOW. Learn the "how" in order to complement the "why" and you'll be able to adapt to the changing field of living the "New

Rich" life no matter what changes take place in our world.

With that, I give you the "how". Start changing your life today, and Tim, thanks again.

George Smolinski, M.D.

Four Hour Physician

Free Time:

Hire A Virtual Assistant And Liberate Your Life

By George Smolinski M.D.
Four Hour Physician

TABLE OF CONTENTS

My Story And Why You Need This Book 1

Chapter Two: What Can Your Virtual Assistant Do For You? 12

Chapter Three: How Can I Afford A Virtual Assistant? 18

Chapter Four: How Do I Hire A Virtual Assistant? 23

Chapter Five: Tips & Best Practices For Working With Your Virtual Assistant 30

Chapter Six: Why You Need A Virtual Assistant NOW 38

Chapter Seven: Tools and Apps to Maximize Your Productivity 41

Bonus Chapter: Get Your Toes Wet With Fiverr 47

The 4 Hour Work Week Tool Box

M‌y Story A‌nd W‌hy You Need T‌his B‌ook

I was trapped.

It seems like an eternity ago now, but a few short years ago, I found myself trapped with, I thought, no way out. Superficially, I was doing great: I was running a medical clinic, had just passed my second board certification exam a short while ago, I was seeing patients and making differences in people's lives, and I was a father to three boys and husband to a fantastic wife. I had worked *extremely* hard to get where I was and I was miserable, and I *could not figure out why.* I could not figure out why it seemed like I was spinning in circles and felt that I had endless task lists that would never be finished. I felt like I needed another two or three of "me" to get everything I needed done.

The worst part was not knowing why. Why was I feeling this way? Then, it all changed, and I finally figured it out. **I was miserable and exhausted because I had built everything to revolve around me, and I didn't have the help I needed to GET THINGS DONE.** Decision making flowed only through me, and left me exhausted. Administrative tasks? Yep, I'd do them too, no matter how trivial. If the devil was in the details, I'd certainly found him, and I felt like I was working myself into an early grave.

But, there was the light I found in reading Tim Ferriss' Four Hour Work Week. I was searching for the "other way", and I found it! Chapter Eight of his book,

The 4 Hour Work Week Tool Box

"Outsourcing Life" hit me like a ton of bricks. I was *floored. These people had all the help they needed and were truly living their lives!* How were they doing it? How were they able to live wherever they wanted around the world? How were they able to actually accomplish the big tasks at work and not have to worry about the minutiae getting done? Two words: Virtual Assistants.

Immediately, I set to work finding myself a Virtual Assistant (VA). It took a lot of work as you'll read about later, but I finally found Angeline, and Angeline changed my life personally and professionally, and has even made our family life better! She's done SO MUCH for me that has allowed me to do some pretty amazing things:

- Travel with my family all over Europe and see the best sites and eat at the best restaurants

- Stay at the most family-friendly ski resorts in the Alps and get my kids set up with ski lessons

- Free up time so that I could compete in all manner of mountain bike races, even managing a couple podium finishes

- Helped me build the business that is Four Hour Physician

The best thing she does, though, is not accomplishing the big tasks like planning a family vacation (though she's more than capable in travel planning!), but getting the small things taken care of so that I don't have to worry about them getting done, and don't have to spend the

The 4 Hour Work Week Tool Box

time doing them. That feeling of having someone there devoted to you and available to rely on is just incredible.

Branching out from Angeline, I thought maybe there were other areas of my life that I could outsource. I needed to write a few articles on medical conditions, so I found a VA to help find applicable journal articles for me to read and use in the articles. Right there I saved close to 5 hours of searching online and sifting through appropriate articles. I contacted the VA and 2 days later I had 10 PDF's of the articles in my inbox! I had given him the title of the article and nothing else, and he'd come up with 10 great articles *while I had been busy doing other things.* **I had found the secret:** *I found someone to do the work I needed to do while I was working on other tasks. I had cloned a part of myself and doubled my productivity.* Amazing!

That brings us to today. By leveraging the best in technology and the best in virtual assistance, I've been able to accomplish the work of two George Smolinski M.D.'s and been able to liberate my life to follow my passions. Now, I get up in the morning, and read on Trello that Doaa is pulling together all of my posts from Four Hour Physician on cloud storage to compose a special report for my subscribers. Angeline in the Philippines has submitted my airline ticket stubs from a recent trip to my United Airlines account, and Jeet in India blew me away with a superb cover design for this eBook. I've found, hired, and worked with over 3 dozen VA's in a wide variety of fields; I'm even a top 10% oDesk client since I've hired so many VA's to do so

The 4 Hour Work Week Tool Box

many tasks for me! **I've replicated what Tim Ferriss has done to supercharge his productivity and my goal now is to help you replicate what I've done so that you too can free your time and liberate your life. Read on to find out how.**

The 4 Hour Work Week Tool Box

CHAPTER ONE: WHAT IS A VIRTUAL ASSISTANT?

In today's business and professional environments, the art of maximizing productivity and efficiency is always a primary concern. Many times business owners and busy professionals can become completely overwhelmed with the various tasks involved in managing their day-to-day operations, causing them to spend more time in "maintenance mode" instead of making actual progress. Keeping an email inbox up-to-date, screening or returning phone calls, managing an appointment calendar, and booking travel arrangements are just a few examples of the kinds of low-value, time-consuming activities that are common to most business professionals. Although these tasks need to be completed, they can put a damper on your ability to focus on the activities that can actually advance your business and in the case of physicians, they negatively impact the time you can spend with patient care. For those of us old enough to remember, 20 or 30 years ago seemingly everyone had a secretary, but now, in the era of "cost cutting", corporations and businesses have eliminated a lot of these positions, foisting these secretarial tasks on the end user: YOU! In essence, this practice has actually reduced our productivity, but thanks to technological advances in the last decade, regaining that vital assistance--through virtual assistance--is now back within our means.

Nineteenth-century Italian economist Vilfredo Pareto introduced a powerful concept known as the Pareto

The 4 Hour Work Week Tool Box

Principle, which states that 80% of your results will come from only 20% of your efforts. Unfortunately, most business owners and professionals end up spending the majority of their time focusing on the 80% of their efforts like email, appointments, etc., that produce little to no long-term results. This happens primarily because they lack the help they need to handle all of the low-value tasks that prevent them from focusing exclusively on the high-value tasks and focusing on their passions. For this reason, hiring a virtual assistant also known as a "VA" is one of the wisest decisions a business owner or any busy professional can make. Indubitably, if you can spend the vast majority of your time on that 20% of your tasks, not only will your income increase, but *your stress level will decrease, as you're spending most of your time being maximally productive and doing what you love!*

But why hire a virtual assistant? The short answer is that they will allow you to focus on doing what you do best and importantly *allow you to focus on what you truly enjoy doing* while they take care of the other activities that you either don't do so well or do not enjoy. Some of the most brilliant, creative and talented business owners, professionals, and physicians in the world will readily admit that they are terrible at keeping track of the administrative aspects of their businesses and practices. However, these folks recognize that their time is valuable, and they choose **not** to spend their time struggling to complete tasks that they either do not do well or do not want to do in the first place. Instead, these wise men and women invest their time performing tasks that play to their strengths and passions, and consequently enlist the help of others to take care of everything else. Hiring a virtual assistant will enable you to adopt that same practice: offload those tasks that you don't perform well or just don't care to perform, enabling you to perform better and focus on your strengths and passions. Virtual assistants free your time to help liberate your life!

I'll use myself as an example of this. I'm the father of four young boys (two still in diapers!), husband, full time physician, entrepreneur, snowboarder and mountain biker. Through utilization of fantastic Virtual Assistants, I've been able to not only do all these things but *do them well*. It does no good to be the person who has 50 irons in the fire, none of which get hot. I'm always looking for new projects and ideas and have an intense creative desire, and by leveraging technology and working with my Virtual Assistants, I can excel in my passions, play to my strengths, and have fun with my life. I've freed my time to liberate my life and that's exactly what I want for you too!

Importantly, virtual assistants also allow rapid scaling of your business. If you have a successful business or medical practice, you're obviously going to have more and more customers or patients that come to call on your services. How can you accommodate this influx, especially in today's climate where information spreads virally and you need to hire more support staff immediately? Virtual assistants, being easy to hire utilizing the methods I describe below, can allow for rapid scaling of your business or practice, allowing you to help these customers and patients effectively and efficiently.

The 4 Hour Work Week Tool Box

I'm also passionate about learning new things that are personally or professionally satisfying for me. Conversely, I definitely don't want to waste my time learning something in detail when only a broad general knowledge of the subject is needed. This is where virtual assistants can help out tremendously as well. A virtual assistant can be extraordinarily beneficial because they have expertise in certain areas that you can leverage to your benefit. They can expertly accomplish tasks that would take you hours, days, or even weeks to not only learn, but become proficient in performing. It has often been said that expertise in a particular skill takes 10,000 hours of performing that skill, whether that's snowboarding, managing people in a leadership role, or performing an appendectomy. Do you have 10,000 hours to learn the expertise needed to establish and run a website? Even less demanding tasks like incorporating video into a PowerPoint presentation take time to learn, and an extremely valuable use of *your* time to do what I do is let someone else with the expertise--a virtual assistant--do these tasks for you.

So what exactly is a virtual assistant? The typical virtual assistant is an independent contractor who performs administrative tasks and provides specialized services to businesses, entrepreneurs and other busy professionals. A virtual assistant usually possesses a solid set of secretarial, technical, clerical, or creative skills that enables them to perform a variety of services to businesses. For the most part, virtual assistants are hired by small and medium sized businesses but even one-person "solopreneurs" can benefit from their skills. Additionally, they are often hired by professionals including physicians, lawyers, management consultants, accountants, stockbrokers, and other specialized occupations. Many businesses choose to utilize the services of a virtual assistant in order to decrease their overhead, as the costs of hiring a full-time employee may prove to be prohibitive when expenses such as payroll tax, health insurance and other factors are taken into consideration. The current economic downturn has indeed ramped up the demand for virtual assistants, since businesses are being forced to employ more creative means to carry on their daily operations, while at the same time keeping costs low.

Virtual assistants are typically referred to as "online virtual assistants" as well, because the primary channels they utilize for communication and data transmission are the Internet (via email, instant messaging, Google Chat, or web conferencing) as well as through the telephone via Voice Over Internet Provider services, such as Skype. Most virtual assistants will also employ the use of web-based data storage and retrieval services like Google Drive, Evernote, and Dropbox in order to facilitate an easy means of sending and receiving important files. In the majority of cases, a virtual assistant is not considered to be your employee in a strict, technical sense; rather, they are considered to be an independent contractor or a consultant that you would hire to work for a certain number of hours per month, have available on an as-needed basis for when tasks arise, or hire just to complete specific projects. This is an additional advantage to businesses as well, because if the relationship doesn't work out, they can terminate the VA

The 4 Hour Work Week Tool Box

without any of the Human Resources headaches that are common to handling employee terminations.

Clearly, a virtual assistant can bring several significant advantages to your business or profession. Aside from the obvious benefit of saving you time with administrative tasks, a virtual assistant can bring a fresh set of eyes to your business, and can even act as a sounding board for your plans and ideas. My personal virtual assistant, Angeline, has helped me on a number of tasks and provided me with truly valuable insights. Most recently, I've had a large project that I've been working on and she, having worked for other entrepreneurs as well, has been able to utilize knowledge gained from her other contracting jobs to help improve my project. Remember, your virtual assistant is an expert in their field, and as such, if there's a particular problem that you, your practice, or your company is facing with a particular issue, there's a great chance that your virtual assistant has seen a similar problem before and can offer helpful advice.

Although hiring a virtual assistant does offer many benefits, this does not mean that all of your problems will be magically wiped away if you hire one. As a matter of fact, without a specific plan set in place to help the virtual assistant understand their role and function within your business, you could end up with even more on your plate. The lack of a well-thought-out strategy to maximize the use of a virtual assistant can produce a situation where you'll be trying to keep your business afloat while simultaneously putting out fires resulting from errors in communication with your virtual

The 4 Hour Work Week Tool Box

assistant. I discuss this quite a bit later on and offer specific tips and guidance to maximize your relationship with your VA, so read on!

The 4 Hour Work Week Tool Box

CHAPTER TWO: WHAT CAN YOUR VIRTUAL ASSISTANT DO FOR YOU?

What can a VA be used for besides what I've discussed above? Obviously, any task that you have that can be done online can be done by a VA. Make a PowerPoint presentation? Sure! Transcribe a podcast into a blog post? Absolutely! Take an audio file and some PowerPoint slides and make a video for YouTube? Definitely! I've had these tasks completed for me using VA's from oDesk with fantastic results. *Here's the bottom line that you absolutely have to remember: your time is valuable so outsourcing ANYTHING you can will be tremendously valuable.* It's safe to say that really anything that can be accomplished online (which is an enormous number of tasks nowadays) can be accomplished by a VA. Please, don't be afraid of outsourcing anything to a VA, especially once you've built a trusting relationship. Obviously don't outsource things that involve your personal information such as credit card numbers, etc., if you're not comfortable doing that, but as I discuss below, there are even workarounds for overcoming that "personal information" obstacle too.

Don't forget about outsourcing personal tasks to your VA as well; Angeline my personal VA does professional and personal tasks for me, accomplishing both with aplomb. For instance, I've had her do a ton of travel planning for me and one of the most useful ways I've found to utilize my VA is to have her help me with travel research. I've never been a fan of travel agents, so from the start, I figured I'd let Angeline try her hand at it. She's been great, but for a business trip that I took recently I

The 4 Hour Work Week Tool Box

somehow turned my brain off and booked my travel myself instead of letting my VA do it. After **hours** of time on travel websites, I had everything planned out. After I had everything booked, my wife promptly told me that I would NOT be doing that again and that my VA should be doing it instead! Right she was. My VA would have saved me dozens of hours, and my lesson has been learned.

You may be worried about giving out credit card information to a VA to book travel plans, and understandably so. The key to any relationship is trust, and, if you've found the right VA for you (hopefully by using my template to find the perfect VA) you'll build up trust to the point of letting him or her book your travel. One nice work-around especially when you first start working with your VA is utilizing a service called LastPass. LastPass allows you to record your credit card information or passwords or any sort of logon information and then give your VA a special key code that will allow him or her to use that credit card or password or login **without letting them see the credit card number, password or login!**

Short of that, even simpler travel tasks can be accomplished by a VA:

- Finding the best restaurants in a city you're visiting--My VA is **GREAT** at this! If we're going on a trip somewhere, I have her find the top restaurants using online review sites, sort the restaurants, and give me the top 3 with

13

The 4 Hour Work Week Tool Box

walking and driving directions to each via Google Maps.
- Get the top hotel recommendations for a given area
- Find out if there are discounts or deals on attractions in a given area during your visit

VA's can be really useful too after a trip. I'm a member of most airline, hotel, and rental car programs. If I neglected to put my frequent flyer or traveler numbers in during my reservation process, I just email photos of the ticket stubs or the reservation to my VA and she requests the miles or points. It's a tremendous time-saver. I've even had my VA request refunds for travel for me, with great success (read below).

Your VA can even take care of the most monumental task ever: Being your first point of contact for email! Why spend time sorting through mountains of emails every day? A very easy strategy would be to use a service like LastPass mentioned above to give your VA access to your email and allow him or her to be the first eyes on any email you receive. It goes without saying that you'll need to work for a while to build that trusting relationship before doing this, but at that point, he or she can be the first responder for your emails. Someone needs to set up a meeting with you? Give your VA access to your Google Calendar account (or other web-based calendar program) and your email, and he or she can coordinate it, freeing you up from the time you'd spend sending 10 back-and-forth emails with the other attendees trying to coordinate a date, time, and location. Getting junk email? Your VA can clean up your inbox for you. Another

The 4 Hour Work Week Tool Box

example: Let's say you get an email saying that your credentials are coming due. Your VA can gather the appropriate paperwork and work with your credentialing office, without you having to chase down years of records. The possibilities are endless!

Here's a list, then, of things that I've personally had my VA do for me or my colleagues have had their VA's accomplish for them:

- Find and purchase items online (Personal example: I had to find specific light bulbs for the license plate light in my Prius. One 30 second email to Angeline, my VA, and they were in my mailbox a week later. I guarantee that was at least a 10 minute task online if I'd done it myself)

- Translate documents from one language to another or simplify complex jargon into easily digestible common parlance

- Submit expense reports and reimbursement requests

- Answer customer questions and complaints

- Send an e-card to business associates on their birthday

- Find the best restaurants in a given area and make reservations

- Request credits for frequent flyer and hotel rewards programs

The 4 Hour Work Week Tool Box

- Track commodity prices

- Conduct medical research for journal articles

- Find a used piano for sale

- Write articles for blog posts

- Build and maintain websites

- Write and submit press releases

- Transcribe audio files

- Listen to webinars and draft executive summaries for you (who has time to listen to an hour webinar or podcast to learn perhaps 3 or 4 important points?)

- Research the most family-friendly ski resorts in Austria

- Take your existing website and optimize it for search engines (SEO)

- Provide driving and/or walking directions to a location via Google Maps

- And, possibly the best leverage technique: Find other VA's to accomplish other tasks that your VA isn't personally familiar with

Take a look at your calendar and pay close attention to the things you do both at work and at home for the next three days, and ask yourself with each and every task, "Is

The 4 Hour Work Week Tool Box

this something a VA could do?" I guarantee you'll come up with an enormous list of things that can be offloaded to a VA.

Chapter Three: How Can I Afford A Virtual Assistant?

At this point, you're probably thinking a VA sounds awesome, but you may be asking, "Can I really afford a virtual assistant?" Later on, I'll give you a personal travel example from my own life about how much a virtual assistant can help you save in terms of both money and, more importantly, time. But before that, I want to you to think long and hard about the question: What is most important to you: Time, Money, or Health? I believe personally that you can always make more money, and you can always improve your health, but you can't create more time, so that leaves time as your most valuable asset.

Therefore, I believe that the most important thing to conserve and treasure is your time, and as such, any method or technique to improve your personal efficiency (and in the process save time) should be included in your daily life. But again, what about the monetary aspect of hiring a VA? Let's be honest, it does cost money to hire a virtual assistant, **but a properly utilized virtual assistant should save you not only your most valuable asset--time--but also save you money.** Here's how my VA did both!

About a year and a half ago my wife and I were set to fly to Mauritius, a tiny island country off the coast of Africa. We had a great vacation planned: we were going to sit on the beach, enjoy some sun, and have a fantastic time relaxing together. We arrived at the airport, went to check in and, when we handed our passports to the

The 4 Hour Work Week Tool Box

airline attendant at the check-in counter, he looked at us and said "Sorry, you're not going to Mauritius today".

As it turns out, you need six months left on your passport before it expires in order to be allowed into Mauritius, and my passport had only five months left before it expired. We had no idea that any of this was going to happen to us, and at first we were devastated. Fortunately we are smart, adaptable people. We got out our iPhones and booked a last minute trip to Malta instead. But, we'd already paid for plane tickets to Mauritius and paid a deposit on a hotel room. We thought we were going to be out this money, but I figured I'd let my virtual assistant try her hand at recovering some of the money.

I sent her all the information I had--it took less than a minute to send her the emails and the receipts that I had for our trip to Mauritius (I had them all archived in Google Drive so sharing them with my VA was a breeze). She took the ball and ran with it, and two weeks later we received a refund for $400 in our bank account from the airline. Granted, we didn't get all the travel expenses reimbursed, but four hundred dollars is four hundred dollars! She worked at it for about 4 hours' time I couldn't afford to spend--and came up with that great result. Obviously, I gave my VA a tip for her hard work and getting us the refund. That's only one example of the things that she has done for me in this same arena of trying to obtain refunds, sending in customer service complaints, and the like. These are things that I just don't have the time to do and offloading them to my VA has been extremely beneficial. Clearly, a VA can save you a ton of time, but they can also save you a ton of money if properly utilized.

One personal touch that I'd like to add is the importance of having a VA for when life throws you a curveball. In March 2013 I had major emergency surgery and although I came through the surgery OK, I was off of work for a MONTH. I have no doubt that having a VA was a key element in keeping my life going, not just for managing tasks, but even having the knowledge that there was a "backstop" to help manage my business tasks when I was laid up in the hospital was HUGE. Think about what would happen if you were in a similar situation. Would you have someone to keep the ship sailing along? Or are you a one-person show, doing everything yourself? As demonstrated by my personal experience, hiring a Virtual Assistant to outsource tasks to is important during your daily life but when life throws you a curveball, you'll DEFINITELY be happy you have a VA to keep the ship afloat.

It bears pointing out here as well that there are both on-shore and off-shore options for hiring a VA and your choice of on-shore vs. off-shore will have a big impact on the expenses you incur when hiring a VA. I've actually had some very interesting discussions over email and on Four Hour Physician regarding this very subject. It can be a hot-button issue, as nobody likes to see jobs lost from American soil. Quite bluntly, off-shore foreign VA's have burst onto the scene in the last few years due to two factors:

    1. They're cheaper than North American or European VA's

The 4 Hour Work Week Tool Box

2. The technological advances in terms of communication, conferencing, and file sharing (think Skype, Google Drive, and Google Hangouts) has allowed effective remote interaction around the world

There's a valid argument that with a North American-based VA, or even one from Europe, you probably start out with a greater chance of hiring someone with excellent command of the English language, which I feel is important because so much of your relationship with your VA depends on communication. However, do you really have the funds to pay up to $25/hour for this assistance?

I would argue, then, that off-shore VA's, who are available at much lower rates (around $5 or $6 per hour), can in fact, be valuable additions to your team, at a fraction of the price that a North American or European VA would cost. I back this claim up with both personal examples as well as examples from my friends and colleagues who have hired off-shore VA's who have done fantastic work for them. *Remember, the absolute, most important factor in finding a VA from ANYWHERE is proper vetting and interviewing of your candidates in order to maximize the chances of hiring someone that will work well with you.* There's a chance that you could find a $25/hour VA who is just plain terrible, and obviously there's also a chance that you could find a $4/hour VA who is just as terrible. However, proper vetting and interviewing will give you that chance to find a truly awesome VA, such as my own VA Angeline, who can

The 4 Hour Work Week Tool Box

accomplish great things for you and your business or medical practice but *not* cost a fortune.

Chapter Four: How Do I Hire A Virtual Assistant?

Now that you understand the "why" of "why you need a VA", I'd like to discuss the "how". Hiring a VA can certainly be intimidating. You may not know where to go, how to sift through candidates, how to properly vet a candidate and conduct an interview, and how to then finalize the deal. This chapter will take you through the "how" from locating suitable candidates to properly conducting the interviews.

The next question you may have is, "Where do I find a VA?" I myself have used oDesk extensively (and exclusively) for the past few years in hiring my own Virtual Assistants, and I think its user-friendly, has literally hundreds of thousands of contractors on it for you to hire, and makes payment easy and automatic. I've used it enough to be in the Top 10% of oDesk Clients, and as such, I've gained a ton of experience using their site. There are a lot of other places online to find Virtual Assistants, such as Elance, another site similar to oDesk. However, "You can only know what you know", and I know oDesk and I know that it works great. If you don't know how to navigate oDesk or have never used it before, I've recorded a two-part training video series that takes you through the ins and outs of oDesk located in my resources.

Once you've found a place that has VA's available to hire, you next need to find the best VA to work with *you*. As I've alluded to above, in the world of virtual outsourcing just as in any field, there is always the chance that you'll run across a terrible VA. As a point of reference, one of my friends hired a VA without really any forethought or interviewing; he just hired the first great resume he read. As you can imagine, that didn't work out well as his VA had barely passable English, had little initiative, didn't pay attention to details, and had difficulty completing even the simplest of tasks. Conversely, I've had friends go through a complete, thorough vetting process based on my recommendations below, and they've been able to hire hard-working, productive, and extremely competent VA's. So, how to mitigate this risk of hiring a dud VA? Here's how to do it:

INITIAL SCREENING

If you want a virtual assistant who is attentive, detail-oriented and assertive, the best initial screening that you can do is to post detailed job application steps with your job description. Think about it: no matter who you want to hire for either a virtual job or an on-site job, you *always* want to have a specific, detailed, and complete job description with the exact parameters of the job spelled out as much as possible. Taking the time to ensure that you have this in place will help weed out candidates who aren't interested in the tasks or position you're offering, and, if you use some tips that I talk about in my own VA Hiring Template, you'll be able to effectively weed out the people who don't pay attention to details--an absolute key personality trait in a Virtual Assistant! As an aside, this template took me nearly 20 hours to formulate, and I used the best templates I could find online and did a ton of research to formulate a solid hiring template, as again, posting a great job description

The 4 Hour Work Week Tool Box

is one of the most important first steps in hiring a superb Virtual Assistant. Next, for those candidates who don't meet your criteria and/or have failed to follow your instructions--including my slick "attention to detail" tip in my VA Hiring Template--they should be eliminated from your list of candidates without a second thought. After this initial culling of candidates who don't meet your criteria and/or don't fulfill this "attention to detail" request, you'll be left with a list of candidates to interview via the two easy steps below.

VIRTUAL ASSISTANT INTERVIEW STEPS

Step One: Interview Via Email

Dubbed as one of the "best practices" for interviewing a VA, an interview via email will give you a glimpse of how a VA is going to interpret and respond to your requests and tasks. You can obviously find out a lot of things about your applicant through e-mail.

Here are some things that you can infer from their writing:

- Ability to read and understand the tasks that you are giving to them

- Ability to read and write proper English

- Degree of being meticulous and detail-oriented

- Availability (are they available Mon-Fri only? or 7 days a week?)

- Skill sets (transcription, Microsoft Office, etc.)

The 4 Hour Work Week Tool Box

To glean this information, here's a complete set of questions to ask in the interview:

- How long have you been working as a virtual contractor?

- What are your previous work experiences (both virtual and in-person employment)?

- What have you learned from these experiences that you can apply to this job when you're working for me?

- What has been your biggest failure as a VA?

- What did you learn from that failure?

- Why are you interested in the job that I've posted?

- What are the skills that you have that you could possibly contribute in order to deliver the best work?

- Do you have any pet peeves?

- Can you send me your portfolio? Note: On oDesk, candidates can upload documents and screenshots to their portfolio, and--great tip here--I would *never hire a VA that doesn't have a portfolio.* Think about it: if you were serious about looking for a job, wouldn't you want to showcase your work?

- Do you have a reliable internet connection?

The 4 Hour Work Week Tool Box

- What is your availability, in terms of hours per day and days per week?

- How many other Virtual Assistant jobs are you performing right now? Note: you don't want a VA that is holding down 10 different VA jobs as their attention to you will be poor!

- What's the best way to communicate with you (Skype, email, IM, chat, Trello, etc.?) Note: This is a tremendously important question, as readily available communication is the most important factor to keep a solid working relationship alive with your VA

These questions are helpful to assess if the applicant is REALLY willing to work hard for you and has the necessary skills in order to accomplish the job. However, an e-mail will not usually give you the most candid version of your applicant. If you want to get to know the real candidate, you could do an interview via chat or video call. *One final insider tip:* Don't be afraid to ask your VA candidates to perform a fairly simple task for you, like uploading a document to Google Drive within a certain (short!) deadline or finding out a certain factoid (For instance: who was the President of the University of Virginia in 1986?). Candidates that are truly serious about working with you will jump on the opportunity to showcase their capabilities and may surprise you with the efficiency and completeness with which they accomplish these tasks! At this point, then, you should have been able to cull unsuitable candidates from your list, leaving you with a short list of candidates to interview via telephone or video.

The 4 Hour Work Week Tool Box

Step Two: Chat, Voice or Video Interview (Skype or Google Hangout)

The Skype or Google Hangout interview is the closest thing to a personal client-to-contractor interview. This will provide you with the candid version of your applicant. An interview via Skype will give you the best glimpse of what your applicant is truly like and how they interact with you. Subjecting the interviewee to video or telephone calls for an interview will show how confident each of your applicants are. During the interview, you'll want to assess how well their spoken English is if you're going to have them doing any personal phone calls for you. If your VA is only working online, there's a good chance that they could have excellent written English with a bit poorer spoken English, so take the job type into consideration when assessing their spoken English skills.

During the interview, you should also assess the reliability of their internet connection. Does you call drop multiple times? Are they grainy if you're doing a video interview? Ensuring first that it's not *your* computer or internet connection causing the problems, if they have this poor of an internet connection, this could negatively impact communication, the foundation of a good relationship with your VA.

Run through the questions above with the VA you're interviewing, even if it seems like you're repeating what you asked in the email interviews. You want to ensure that their answers are the same, and additionally, you'll be able to assess how well they react to being pressed for information. One outstanding tip for conducting these interviews is to do the following: While you're talking,

The 4 Hour Work Week Tool Box

draft a quick document, writing 2-3 sentences on any subject, put it on Google Drive, and make a fairly obvious spelling error in it. Tell the interviewee that you're going to share the document with them and, while you're talking, you want them to find the error, correct it, and have them re-share the corrected document with you. You can do the same thing with emailing the document back-and-forth or doing it over Evernote or Dropbox as well. This will allow you to assess how well your VA works multi-tasking, especially in the rather high pressure situation of being in a job interview while having to pay attention to detail and correct a typo!

Now, to be 100% honest here, in hiring Angeline, my VA, I did NOT conduct a Skype interview. I've been extremely fortunate to have found her, but in retrospect, it was rather foolhardy to hire her without a Skype interview. DEFINITELY do a Skype or Google Hangout interview before hiring!

In closing, the best way to look at interviewing your VA candidates is to look at it like you would for hiring any other contractor or employee. You want to be clear, up-front, and ensure that the person you're going to hire meets all of your criteria, has excellent attention to detail, and a strong command of the English language. By using the interview questions above to guide you, you should have great success in finding a great VA!

Chapter Five: Tips & Best Practices For Working With Your Virtual Assistant

Finally, I'd like to give you a few tips and "best practices" regarding how to work with your VA so that you can forge a solid working relationship. The first tip has to deal with setting deadlines. I've read the following elsewhere and it makes sense: if you have a project, ANY project, you have to set a deadline and it has to be short. For instance, I give my VA usually 24-48 hours to accomplish any task, with maybe one additional day for high-complexity tasks. Think about it: if you have a task that's due in 3 weeks or 3 days, which one do you focus on first? Obviously the 3 day task gets your attention most of the time. Anything with a long-term deadline is rather difficult to accomplish as it always seems "so far away" and inevitably gets put off for the future. If you add on the fact that your VA may be halfway around the world without direct in-person oversight, setting short and definitive deadlines is highly effective to help accomplish tasks.

The follow-on question becomes: what about those big tasks that take a few weeks to complete? The answer is that you accomplish those just like you'd eat an elephant: one bite at a time. Take the big task and cut it into several manageable chunks and then set short deadlines for each of those tasks. You'll find you eventually *do* accomplish the big task at hand by doing it one bite at a time and you can additionally see and measure progress made towards the completion of the larger task.

The 4 Hour Work Week Tool Box

Next, you will need to learn how to delegate effectively. Back in the day as a medical resident, I didn't delegate anything (this was compounded by the fact that as interns and residents, we didn't have anyone to delegate to!). It was rather horrible, as there was a lot of "scut work" which was really "non value added work". It contributed little to my medical education and was essentially pointless. Fortunately, I had an educational background experience prior to medical school that equipped me with the skills of effective delegation and I would employ these skills in the near future as a staff physician. I learned these skills back in college when I was in charge of a 10K competitive running race--an enormous undertaking, especially given the fact that although I was a runner, I had no clue about what a race director really does. During this trial-by-fire, I learned first-hand that I could NOT do everything, and that I needed a lot of help with the smaller tasks so that I could focus on the bigger tasks.

Fast forward to the first days of being a staff physician, where I immediately went to work finding personnel to help offload my clinic's smaller management tasks, so that I could focus on the big tasks of leading the clinic and immersing myself in patient care. In essence, I quickly became an expert at working smarter, not harder, and I'd like to think that everyone in the clinic benefitted. Not only was I able to focus on the important tasks that I spent nearly a decade to learn, but my support staff learned that they had a very important, key role in keeping the clinic running smoothly and the patients received excellent care, delivered efficiently. Everyone is happy if they feel they can make a solid contribution to

The 4 Hour Work Week Tool Box

a cause every day at work, and by properly delegating tasks, you can not only work smarter, not harder, but also build your team to work towards a common goal, which is a huge morale booster. So, I encourage you to learn to "let go" of the smaller tasks that your VA can handle and build your "team". Only through delegation of tasks can you possibly utilize your VA effectively. If you're uncomfortable with delegation, I'd recommend starting out with delegating small tasks that can be easily accomplished, like making restaurant reservations. Over time, you'll become more and more comfortable with delegation and be able to delegate larger and larger tasks, which in the end, will liberate your perfect life!

Another "best practice" when working with your VA deals with the specificity of tasks. Any task you delegate to your VA must be absolutely crystal clear, and you *must* ask them to ask you questions regarding the task *before* they start work on it. Think about it: when someone gives you a job to do with clear direction and clearly defined parameters, doesn't that make it far easier to accomplish? Here's two examples, one of a poorly defined task for a VA, and one of a well-defined task:

- Poorly Defined Task: "I need you to find me the best Asian restaurant in New York City and get me a reservation for myself and my friends next Saturday" (Side note: if you actually went through and gave *anyone* this task, they'd invariably fail miserably)

- Well Defined Task: "In the next 48 hours (i.e. by noon (Eastern Standard Time), Friday, June 21st) I need you to find me the top 3 Asian fusion

> restaurants in both SoHo and Tribeca, email me the list of the 6 restaurants, and after I pick the one I want to go to, I'll email you back with my selection. I need you to then make a reservation for 3 people at 8 PM for Saturday, July 27th and forward me the confirmation details and forward the details as well to Joe Smith (joesmith@email.com) and Rose Carlson (rosecarlson@email.com), the other two people dining with me on the 27th"

Setting precise goals and definitive deadlines for specific tasks for your VA will be extremely beneficial, as clear communication forms the foundation for any relationship, much less one that is being conducted across the internet halfway around the world. Additionally, you'll need to learn to "let go" and delegate tasks effectively. But communication and delegation is not enough. What are the other "best practices" to forge that solid working relationship? To help answer that question, I went right to the source and I asked my own VA, Angeline, to give me her thoughts and ideas regarding working with VA's, so that you might have a better idea on the best ways to work with your own VA. Here's what she had to say:

You need to PRIORITIZE so that you can reach your goals. You need to eliminate many of the jobs that are not cost effective for you to perform – in other words, you have to cross out some things from your to-do lists and learn to delegate. Why would you do some menial tasks that are clearly hindering you from doing the most important things to improve your career or business?

The 4 Hour Work Week Tool Box

It is indeed a fact that most of you are afraid to delegate tasks because you think that only YOU can do those things right. However, each time you do a mindless task yourself you make a statement about the value of your time. Always remember the basic rule in running your own business: learn to reinvest your earnings back into your career and your business if you want to see progress. Remember, there are two types of tasks you do for your business: basic management tasks and money making tasks. The more basic management tasks you can delegate and offload, the more time you will have to spend making money, and the more you will be able to reinvest in your business and see it grow. As such, in your own case, hire someone like ME - a personal assistant to work on your minor tasks so that you can focus more on your own BIG GOALS.

A virtual assistant is an independent contractor who provides administrative services to clients while operating outside of the client's office through phone, email or instant messages using different internet platforms. A VA usually works off-site, but is still able to have access to the necessary documents required to keep the business running via the internet. Utilization of VA's has become more prominent because of the nature of the off-site VA's contract. Off-site VA contracts for overseas VAs relieves the client from paying the monthly office's rents, equipment and benefits required by the law as opposed to the benefits and rights that are necessitated by full-time onsite personal assistants.

Yes, we know that ONLY YOU can make and meet your own expectations. We also know that you are the boss

The 4 Hour Work Week Tool Box

and that you are always right. But you've got to learn to trust and delegate the tasks that are not part of your major goals. Having a virtual assistant will save you time, money and headaches. We, the VA's are like virtual superheroes and we can work with you to help you reach your goals if you follow some of these guidelines:

1. We can make your life more convenient by booking your tickets, hotel rooms and meeting appointments. But you're definitely missing a lot when you just LIMIT the usual tasks to your VA. Most virtual assistants are highly educated and are skilled in various areas like customer service, content writing, lead generation, human resources, social media, marketing, event planning and research. Make use of their skills that are necessary to your career or business. You will be surprised that some of them can work magic!

2. Always be available. One downside of offsite virtual assistance is the absence of constant communication between the assistant and the boss. Sometimes, time differences can be a hindrance too. But having multiple lines of communication such as email, Skype and other instant messaging business channels helps. Make use of these tools.

3. Set your deadlines, priorities and expectations clearly with your VAs. Explain to them your reasons why these are tasks are important and urgent. However, you will also need to give your VAs the chance to agree, refuse and voice

The 4 Hour Work Week Tool Box

their opinions regarding your standards. Giving us this privilege to form an opinion and share them to you makes us feel important and respected. And in that way, you could both come up with something that is more agreeable and you'll both work more efficiently on the project at hand.

4. Be considerate. Most off-site employees are based in Asia – particularly from the Philippines, India or China. As a Philippine based VA, I can attest that the internet connection in this country is pretty terrible. Internet connections and the electrical power usually perform the best disappearing acts in Asia – this happens a lot during the rainy season in our area. So, if your VA suddenly lost contact with you, please bear with them. [Side note: Angeline had one instance for 3 days where her internet went out but this has been the only time she's had internet issues with me during our long relationship]

5. And lastly, positive reinforcement works well with us. A genuine appreciation and sometimes a token, in a form of bonus or tip could boost our confidence and our desire to deliver the best work for you.

We all understand that a long distance professional relationship is never easy. It needs a lot of time, patience, practice and an internet connection to make it work. But a virtual assistant can definitely save you time, money, and possibly your career one day.

The 4 Hour Work Week Tool Box

These are great tips from Angeline on how to work with a VA from a VA's perspective. I think she's spot on with her tips, and my personal take on these tips is that working with a VA is essentially the same as working with anyone else in your office, with the added twist of doing it online. I would add that getting feedback from your VA is very important as well, as it will help build that solid relationship, if nothing more than by learning how you both communicate best. In summary, if you use the same rules about treating on-site office staff with your VA, i.e. use the Golden Rule, and treat your VA well, he or she can help maximize your time so that you can unlock and liberate the perfect life inside you.

At this point, you've seen that a Virtual Assistant can truly change your life, and therefore I'll offer this: On the Four Hour Physician website, we're now offering a service that will work with you in order to find you the best Virtual Assistant candidates on oDesk and deliver their profiles right to your inbox. The VA Locator Service takes your input on what type of job you're hiring your VA to do, your preferences regarding skills and characteristics that you want in a VA, filters through the hundreds of thousands of candidates on oDesk, and then delivers the best 3 candidates for your position right to your inbox. We're so confident that we can find a great VA for you that we even offer a 100% money back guarantee.

Chapter Six: Why You Need A Virtual Assistant NOW

Today modern medicine in America is at a crossroads. As you can read in my resources, physicians are leaving the practice of medicine in droves—up to a quarter of physicians are planning on leaving medicine in the next year--and this is a trend that is expected to continue. Unfortunately, many of these physicians are leaving medicine because they have been forced to do numerous non-value-added tasks and additionally, have had an increasing number of regulations placed on their practices. So, there's a 1 in 4 chance that if you're a physician reading this eBook, you're planning on leaving your practice, and most likely not because you don't like caring for patients, but because you hate the extraneous details needed in today's day and age.

If you're not a physician and reading this book, you're probably overworked, stressed out, and looking for a solution as well. Physicians are busy, but in this day and age of 80 or even 100 hour workweeks, we all put in countless hours and many of those hours are spent doing those non-value added tasks. They appear in whatever field you're in, whether that's being an entrepreneur, lawyer, dentist, small business owner, etc.

So, what is the solution? I certainly am not naive enough to think that complex problem like overwork and physician burnout can be solved simply, but I believe that a partial solution can be found in outsourcing the minutiae of life to virtual assistants. Everyday tasks as I described above can be easily outsourced to virtual assistants. In my own case, outsourcing these types of tasks has proven *extremely* beneficial, as it has left me time to see patients more effectively as well as pursue my passions outside of work. The same applies to any field or any business—the more you can outsource the small tasks, those more you'll be able to apply yourself to the big, important tasks.

I'll be perfectly honest: The life that I had built as I describe in the introduction where I describe myself as "trapped" was horrendous. It was bad enough for me to consider leaving the practice of medicine altogether--not a light decision given the decades of education I'd had to reach that point! But, I can say without hyperbole that finding and hiring a virtual assistant changed my life. I cannot emphasize enough how having that "extra set of hands" to take care of the day-to-day tasks of my life so that I could concentrate on my patients, my family, and my passions truly liberated my life. Now, I'm satisfied and content. I used to be one of those 25% of physicians contemplating leaving medicine, and now I'm staying in for the long haul.

Let me help you find the same satisfaction. My goal is to help everyone find a great virtual assistant to help them liberate their lives. You can do this in two ways:

1. Use all of the tools and tips I've given you here and find your own VA

2. Let me do the hard work for you with my Virtual Assistant Locator Service

The 4 Hour Work Week Tool Box

This is not a sales pitch. If I've done it on my own, you can do it too and I've given you all the tools you need. However, I've heard time and time again that the biggest sticking point for people to actually start working with a VA is undergoing the process itself of finding one. As one of my friends said, "I don't have time to make myself efficient!" That's where I can help you. I can remove this large obstacle--finding a great virtual assistant--through the <u>VA Locator Service</u>, which will deliver 3 great VA candidates right to your inbox in a week. It's simple to use and is the best way to get started with a VA immediately.

If you're unsure about a VA to handle a wide range of tasks, I've also created a <u>"Task Specific Virtual Assistant Locator Service"</u>. This service will find you a specific VA to do a specific task, like social media promotion, blog article writing, transcription, or really quite anything! I've hired so many VA's to do so many different tasks, that I can virtually guarantee I can find one to do anything you need done.

Use the tools here or let me help you. Stop wasting your time. Don't leave the practice of medicine. Make the change you need in your life: Get a VA, find happiness again, and liberate your life!

The 4 Hour Work Week Tool Box

CHAPTER SEVEN: TOOLS AND APPS TO MAXIMIZE YOUR PRODUCTIVITY

Effective leveraging of technology is essential to working in that strong relationship with your VA. To that end, I've compiled a list of the most effective programs, tools, and apps out there to help you maximize your relationship with your VA. The links in the text lead to my reviews of them on Four Hour Physician for more details on each tool and I hope you find the tools as useful as I do!

- Trello Project Management Program and App: Trello is a nifty, easy-to-use, FREE web-based program with a complementary iPhone, iPad, and Android app. It's extremely easy to learn and you can easily manage the various tasks you assign to your VA with in-program (and in-app) messaging, checklists, and it even interfaces with Google Drive. I use it with my VA's to coordinate efforts on projects, and it's great to wake up and see 5 new Trello notifications alerting me that my VA's have made progress on our projects.

- oDesk Virtual Staff & Freelancer Website: oDesk is the site that I used to hire my first Virtual Assistants, and I have used oDesk for years. There are other online freelancer sites out there with Virtual Assistants ready for hiring such as Elance, but I started with oDesk years ago and I've been happy with them ever since. I think their website is very easy to navigate; it's extremely easy to not only pay

The 4 Hour Work Week Tool Box

your VA's but give them tips and bonuses, and they are, in fact, the largest freelancer site in the world.

- iWriter: A big argument is that with "micro-VA" jobs, often times you pay up front and then if you're stuck with an unsatisfactory end product, you're out that money. I've had this happen to me personally, but in my opinion, nothing ventured, nothing gained. A great way around this specifically for writing tasks is to use an author from iWriter. The great thing is that an iWriter author will write an article or ebook for you (note that this ebook is 100% George Smolinski!) and you have 72 hours to review the content. If you like it, you pay, and if you don't you can request a re-write. Authors compete for your jobs, and I've had good articles written for under $5!

- JustHost: JustHost is the hosting company that I myself have used for Four Hour Physician since its inception, and I've been very pleased with their hosting and the ease of use of their site. It's quick and easy to access all of the functions you need through the "CPanel" control panel page, which is the default page that you're brought to when you log in. From there, building your site is easy using Wordpress, Weebly, or Simple Scripts. Also, accessing webmail for your site, setting up autoresponders and forwarders for email addresses, and managing your domains is all quick one-click access, without the need to know specialized programming language. Since JustHost is such a large hosting provider, your VA should be familiar with it and it will be easy for them to use should you want to set up a website for your business or practice.

- Onavo Extend and Onavo Monitor Smartphone Apps: Extend and Monitor by Onavo give you the ability to use the data on your smartphone longer, and keep track of how much data you're using. Both work great, but Extend actually compresses your data so that you get more data each month on your smartphone. Onavo Monitor tracks your data usage so you don't go over your data plan in any given month. The best part? They're FREE!

- Google Drive Cloud Storage: If you're not using Google Drive, you're missing out on one of the best FREE cloud storage programs out there. Its slick, integrates with Gmail, and works well across PC and Mac platforms. I've used it for years and my VA's share documents, PowerPoints, and Excel spreadsheets with me via Google Drive on an almost-daily basis.

- Evernote Cloud Storage: Another big dog in the cloud storage world, Evernote is similar to Google Drive but its iPhone app is better and it has (for premium users) the ability to actually search for text within photos and PDF's without opening them up! It's truly magical and definitely a great program that can be

The 4 Hour Work Week Tool Box

accessed on your computer, on the web, or on your smartphone. I've set up a shared folder in Evernote that my VA, Angeline, uses to share documents with me and it works great.

- Dropbox Cloud Storage: The last of the big three in cloud storage. Dropbox a great program again with highly functional apps for Android and iPhones/iPads. It's very user friendly and perhaps a bit more intuitive than Evernote but sadly lacks the "in-photo" text searching which again is an amazing Evernote feature. It's used extensively in the cloud storage world, however, and many VA's utilize it with their clients.

- Skype: Admittedly, Skype can sometimes be a bit buggy, but in terms of the most widely used VOIP programs out there, Skype is it. The iPhone app is fairly user-friendly, and we even have a Skype phone in our house. I would NOT, however, use Skype for any sort of dictation! I've had calls dropped, and when you're doing a dial-in dictation and have been dictating for 20 minutes and the call is dropped and you lose all your work--well, that's just about enough to make you want to throw your iPhone against a wall. So, keep the conversations short and you should be quite pleased.

- Google Hangouts: Google Hangouts is an extremely useful tool that I've used with my own VA's to help train them on doing certain

The 4 Hour Work Week Tool Box

tasks online. You can screenshare with the other people on the Hangout and even use the remote desktop function to go into their desktop and control their computer! A great bonus is the ability to record the session which is then saved to your YouTube account. This makes a handy reference tool then, for specific tasks that you teach your VA that they can easily access in the future.

- Lastpass: As I talked about before, Lastpass is a fantastic tool that simplifies password management. Before, I had used a private folder for my passwords on my computer: NOT SAFE. Discovering Lastpass was extremely fortuitous, as it stores passwords securely using the absolute best in secure password management. You can also share an individual logon for any website with your VA, allowing them to access your account on any site *without seeing your password*. How great is that?

- TripIt Travel Itinerary Manager: I'm a huge fan of TripIt's Pro service, having used the free basic service provided by TripIt for years. TripIt is a useful, intuitive web-based itinerary manager that has a correspondingly useful app for iPhones, iPads and Android. There are two options to get your itinerary into TripIt, either manually (slow and painful) or by letting TripIt scan your email and then build itineraries right from the emails which works

45

The 4 Hour Work Week Tool Box

amazingly well. TripIt Pro has some great features that make it worth the $49/year fee, in my opinion. These include free Hertz Club Gold membership (great time saver--your car is waiting for you and you jump in and drive away!), flight alerts that can be sent to your smartphone or email for flight changes, and a Seat Tracker feature that alerts you via email or text if a better seat becomes available on your flights. The biggest benefit, though, is auto-sharing your itineraries with whomever you designate. If you've taken my advice and let your VA manage your calendar and travel, this feature is invaluable to let them work most effectively for you.

In closing, you've now been exposed to all the tools necessary to find, interview, and hire a Virtual Assistant. You've seen how these "virtual superheroes" can literally change your life and make an impact on your personal life, your professional life, your practice, and your business. We live in a remarkable world with amazing tools that now allow us to work smarter than ever before. I encourage all of you to take the plunge and leverage these tools to hire your own Virtual Assistant, free your time, and liberate your life.

The last thing I'll ask you is to please leave a review of this book on Amazon if you've found **any** of this information helpful; you can find the book by following this link. Thanks so much!

Bonus Chapter: Get Your Toes Wet With Fiverr

Admittedly, many people are intrigued with the concept of a virtual assistant but for a variety of reasons are somewhat hesitant to hire one. I recently conducted a poll on Twitter asking people what barriers they faced with hiring a VA and some of the first responses that came in showed that people were unsure if a VA could truly help them and were worried about "taking the plunge".

I thought about this scenario and I can certainly see how one might be intimidated by the prospect of jumping in with both feet and hiring a VA to help them out; after all, it's a virtual ocean of talented contractors, so where to start? I have a **great** solution for you if you're one of those people: instead of jumping in the deep end, get your toes with a neat micro-VA site that I love called Fiverr.

Fiverr's concept is extremely interesting. You sign up for an account and you're brought to a fairly simple site with a broad range of task categories listed, the vast majority of which are simple "one off" tasks. You pay $5 for the given task, which can be anything from the most zany (draw a picture of a chicken on paper, roast the paper and mail the "roasted" chicken to you) to the most vanilla (transcribe any video up to 10 minutes in length). One thing to note is that the base price for these tasks is $5 but many tasks have additional features that you can purchase in $5 increments, such as rush delivery.

The 4 Hour Work Week Tool Box

You communicate with your micro freelancer exclusively within Fiverr's message system which is very easy to use, and any task that you hire a contractor for has an approximate due date. As such, it's very simple to use:

1. Choose a task to be done, known as a "gig" on Fiverr

2. Find a contractor to do it

3. Hire them and pay the $5 via PayPal or credit card

4. If required by the contractor, provide additional information for the task (you'll get a message in your email linked to Fiverr and in your Fiverr message center if this is the case)

5. Wait until the task is completed—you'll get an email indicating this and a message in the Fiverr message center

I've personally used Fiverr for creating ebook covers, some SEO strategy, and other assorted small jobs and found it pretty useful. Here's a real life example of the quality of work you can obtain on Fiverr: I had the cover of this eBook designed by a Fiverr contractor and he completed it using his own artistic talent (I provided him the text) and had it back to me in a week! It was delivered right to my Fiverr message box ready for uploading to the Amazon Kindle publication page. Having used it a lot, I can safely say that just like with oDesk the best way to get a quality product is to hire a contractor that has great

The 4 Hour Work Week Tool Box

reviews. Note as well that when you search for a given task Fiverr will bring up the "Recommended" contractors. They may not be the best for your task! Search by "High Rating" instead and pick the contractor with the most 5 star ratings. Now, you do pay up front for the "gig" on Fiverr so if you get a bad final product, you're out that $5. I have gotten burned on poor quality final products but this has been less than 10% of the time, and my personal opinion is a 90% success rate for $5 tasks is pretty great.

So, why start out with Fiverr when you're just starting to work with VA's? Simple: It's a great way to not only get tasks accomplished for a low price, but it's also an *excellent* way to build up your experience with delegating tasks to a VA. That concept of delegating a task to someone who may live halfway around the world is sometimes a big barrier to overcome that holds people back from utilizing VA's. But, gaining practice doing it through Fiverr will allow you to become more and more comfortable with it. Remember, however, that you need to **track and analyze what works and what doesn't when you delegate your tasks**. It does NO GOOD to make the same mistakes over and over again so use these task delegations to your "micro VA's" in Fiverr as learning experiences and soon you'll be an excellent delegator!

The 4 Hour Work Week Tool Box

Cloud Watching

A Review of The Best Cloud Storage Programs

George Smolinski M.D.

Four Hour Physician

The 4 Hour Work Week Tool Box

TABLE OF CONTENTS

Chapter One: My Paperwork Disaster 52

Chapter Two: Dropbox 54

Chapter Three: Google Drive + Google Drive/Email Tricks 57

Chapter Four: Amazon Cloud Drive 61

Chapter Five: Evernote 64

Chapter Six: Comparison of Cloud Storage Programs & Recommendations 68

The 4 Hour Work Week Tool Box

Chapter One: My Paperwork Disaster

Three years ago, my office and my "filing system" at home was a disaster. I had papers everywhere and whenever I needed to find some document, I'd spend five or even ten minutes shuffling through papers to try and find it. As I thought about this issue, *I realized I was wasting my life looking for documents!* I then made the decision to leverage technology to solve this problem, and looking into cloud storage solutions. At this point, looking back to that era of my life, I can honestly say that I don't know how I survived! I was so inefficient that it's rather embarrassing, especially when I compare that time to now, where I simply go to any computer in our house or even my smartphone and find whatever file I need.

Here's an example of how powerful cloud storage can be for you: Last week I was walking to the gym and my wife called me and said she was at the bank and needed a particular document. I found it on my iPhone, shared it with her, and she could conduct her business. It took me about 45 seconds to find and share it, and *she* didn't have to go home, find it, and go back to the bank with it. This is the power of cloud storage, a power you should harness to free your time and liberate your life!

So, what is cloud storage? Cloud storage, online storage, and virtual drive, all these terms refer to the storage space available on the internet that is dedicated to depositing users' data—documents, spreadsheets, videos, photos, PowerPoints, etc.--instead of keeping these data on physical storage devices. It has become of

52

The 4 Hour Work Week Tool Box

paramount importance to our business and personal lives, as not only does it allow data backup, but also it allows syncing data across several computers and mobile devices, and provides a convenient environment for collaboration through data sharing between users. Amongst the available cloud storage services today, there are four services that have proved their efficiency and are the most well-known and in the widest use; Google Drive, Dropbox, Amazon Cloud Drive, and Evernote. In this ebook I'm going to review the major characteristics of each of these four services, and then I'll give you a detailed comparison of them, showing their relative strengths and weaknesses. As a final note, I do not have any affiliation with any of these companies to promote the purchase of these cloud storage programs, so rest assured, this review 100% unbiased.

The 4 Hour Work Week Tool Box

Chapter Two: Dropbox

Dropbox is a widely known online data backup service that enables you to sync your data across various computers and mobile devices, and to share files, photos, and videos.

What makes Dropbox really superb is being powerful and efficient, yet very streamlined and user-friendly with a very intuitive interface. And like other cloud storage services, Dropbox allows you to sync data across different operating systems; if each one of the end users has Windows, Mac, or Linux operating system, a special Dropbox folder is created on each hard drive, and all data are synced automatically.

You can share your data with other Dropbox users through email invitations. The shared data appears in their Dropbox, and syncs to their computers automatically. And even if you need non-Dropbox users to gain access to your data, you can send them a link to specific files and folders, which makes Dropbox perfect for team projects (even husband and wife teams!). Also, if you need to access your files from someone else's computer, simply log in to www.dropbox.com. You can view, download, and upload your files securely from any web browser.

After signing up with Dropbox, the program creates a special folder on your computer. To use Dropbox, you simply drop files in your Dropbox folder and they will instantly appear on all of your other computers and the Dropbox web portal for your account. You can make

The 4 Hour Work Week Tool Box

folders in Dropbox, allowing for easy categorization of your files.

Sharing data is also pretty easy; all you need to do is to right click on the desired item on the web or in your local Dropbox folder, and choose "Share Link", and the recipient has full read-only access to the shared item where they can freely view and download the files. But if you need to collaborate on certain files or folders with others, use the "Sharing" option (the little rainbow icon on the left in the screenshot above) in order to provide full read and write access for the end users.

Another useful feature of Dropbox is the ability to restore deleted files. This extends to 30 days after deletion, so that if any item is accidentally deleted, just click on "Show deleted files" and you can restore any deleted item within 30-day period. So, if you're at all worried about accidentally deleting a file that you really actually needed, you may find this feature of Dropbox quite intriguing.

Dropbox offers 2 GB free storage space, which is meager by today's standards; but still you can boost it: you get 250 MB bonus once you have finished 5 items out of the 7-item Dropbox "Get Started" checklist. Also, you can gain extra 500 MB for every person you refer to Dropbox, and extra 125 MB for tweeting about how you find the service useful. And the paid versions are as follows:

1- Pro version: 100 GB at $9.99 monthly or $99 yearly

2- 200 GB at $19.99 monthly or $199 yearly

The 4 Hour Work Week Tool Box

3- 500 GB at $49.99 monthly or $499 yearly.

The best option obviously is to choose to pay per year and enjoy the 17% discount for any of the paid schemes. One interesting option is the Packrat feature for $39 per year. This feature allows you to store unlimited number of deleted files and old versions of your data.

For mobile devices, other than the ease of sharing files and uploading photos and videos, Dropbox provides some distinctive features for specific platforms: with Android and Kindle Fire you can edit Dropbox files. Additionally, with iPhone and iPad offline viewing is possible for Dropbox files that have been added to your Favorites.

Now, let's talk about security. As you may recall, Dropbox was hacked in 2012, whereupon it implemented two-factor authentication. In addition to the improved internal monitoring imposed on storing and sharing users' data, Dropbox sends an email to you seeking your verification prior to sharing any of your information. Also, you get an email notification if another user adds to or changes your data.

But there is one downside, which is absence of the ability to edit or preview Office documents. This ability would save much of the user's time, effort, and storage space as it'd be possible to preview or edit a document without downloading it. Also, sharing photo albums still needs some improvement. Although it can be done, this is one area where Dropbox should work on to improve.

Chapter Three: Google Drive + Google Drive/Email Tricks

If you have a Google account, you can make use of this tremendous service; it's worth it to sign up with the Google *just* to get this service. With Google Drive you can create and store a lot of different file types. It is based off of Microsoft Office, so you have the same types of documents that you find in Office: Word docs, PowerPoints, Excel spreadsheets, and you also can create Forms and Drawings. In addition, you can store PDF's, audio files, and video files using Google Drive.

With Google Drive you can create a Word Doc, Excel spreadsheet, or other Office file, and when you open the file, the default setting is to open it in Google Drive's own version of that Office program. As an aside, Google Drive constantly saves your data on the Drive. This all then works very well because you can do everything online without having to open up the Office program, save the file, and then re-upload it to the cloud. It's also pretty easy to sync across your work computer, home computer, and your smart phone.

The other thing that is really useful about Google Drive is that you can share documents easily; you can share anything that you have on Google Drive with other people really easily but it definitely helps if they have Google accounts. A nice feature of Google Drive is that you can share documents via Facebook and Twitter as well as through Gmail and through Drive. I'm not sure how many people use Twitter as a file-sharing platform,

The 4 Hour Work Week Tool Box

so I'd say these options aren't tremendously useful overall.

Google gives you a fair amount of storage: you get 15 GB free which is shared across Google Drive, Gmail, and Google photos. This certainly could be sufficient if you clean out your storage on a fairly regular basis. Furthermore, you can use Google Drive to increase your Gmail storage by archiving your messages from your Gmail account into your Google Drive account. There is a great tool developed by Marcello Scacchetti at Jellybend that automatically archives your Gmail messages in Google Drive in three easy steps:

1. You're going to make a copy of the script file via copying a spreadsheet into Google Drive.

2. Initialize & authorize the program.

3. Locate the Archive tab in any email and click it. Presto! Sent to Google Drive!

Moreover, Digital Inspiration tech blog shared a Google script that provides the possibility of automatically saving Gmail image attachments to your Google Drive. Also, it scans older emails for images and pulls them out, helping you avoid sifting through tons of older emails searching for specific images.

Deploying procedure is pretty easy: after opening the script in Google Drive, choose File -> Make a copy in order to make a copy of the script in your Drive.

The 4 Hour Work Week Tool Box

Afterwards, click Run -> Authorize. This is essential for the script to be able to read your Gmail Inbox, create Drive Folder and write files into it.

After granting the needed permissions, click Run -> Start Program. Now the script is activated, it creates a "Gmail Images" folder in your Google Drive, and there you'll find your image attachments.

Upon receiving a new email, the script scans the message for image attachments, which will then be automatically sent to the Gmail Images folder. And the script adds a "Processed" label to older image attachments in order to skip them in the next iteration.

In addition to scanning attachments for images, this script can also scan for documents. This can easily be done by modifying the search query in Google Script

Getting back to storage space, if you need more storage space you can choose one of the following quite affordable monthly plans.

- 25 GB for $2.49
- 100 GB for $4.99
- 200 GB for $9.99
- 400 GB for $19.99
- 1 TB for $49.99
- 2 TB for $99.99

The 4 Hour Work Week Tool Box

- 4 TB for $199.99

- 8 TB for $399.99, and

- 16 TB for $799.99 to be shared across Google Drive, Picasa, and additional, but separate, Gmail storage.

Nevertheless, Google Drive does fall a little bit short specifically with PowerPoint presentations however. If you need to actually work on a PowerPoint presentation you're better off storing it on Google Drive and then downloading it to whatever computer you're working on and then working on it locally on that computer. I myself have found that if I try to work on a PowerPoint presentation on Google Drive, the format gets screwed up 6 ways from Sunday. Plus, if you ever try to present right from Google Drive, you're going to look foolish because the different text sizes, the fonts, and/or alignment of the different text bullets is just a mess. So it's useful for storing but it's not useful for actually working on PowerPoint presentations. However, being powered by the most dominant force in the internet today, **The Google**, it's undergoing constant revisions and improvements to make it even better and more user-friendly.

Chapter Four: Amazon Cloud Drive

Being powered by Amazon.com, the most popular e-commerce company in the world, Amazon Cloud Drive has proved to be a robust competitor of all the cloud storage services available so far including Google Drive, Dropbox and Evernote. It has some good features, but as I'll explain, its best used as a photo storage tool, but not for business applications.

Just like all other cloud storage services, upon signing up with Amazon it creates a special folder on your computer, in which you drop files that you want to store on the cloud. The service syncs them across all your computers and mobile devices, and allows you to share files or folders.

When you click "Share", you'll be given a link to the item that you want to share, and this item will be shared only with people having this link and as such your information is only shared with the people you want. Then, by clicking "Stop sharing" you can suspend sharing certain items.

To stop sharing, you can either choose "Stop sharing", or click on "Shared Files", and then check the item you want, and click on "More Actions", that will bring up some options that include "Stop sharing", and "Share again" which you can choose if you have accidentally stopped sharing an item.

The 4 Hour Work Week Tool Box

In addition to the 5 GB free storage space, there are several paid, though cost-effective, schemes for Amazon Cloud:

- **20 GB** for $10 a year
- **50 GB** for $25 a year
- **100 GB** for $50 a year
- **200 GB** for $100 a year
- **500 GB** for $250 a year
- **1000 GB** for $500 per year

For music lovers, there is the **Cloud Player Free** that offers 250 imported songs. And the **Cloud Player Premium** that offers 250,000 imported songs for only **$24.99** a year.

Now let's talk about security. Due to Amazon site being originally oriented toward online purchasing, creating an account involves revealing quite a bit of personal information. Moreover, the website still has major security loopholes, and is vulnerable to be, for example, attacked by XML signature wrapping and cross scripting, as well as uncovered security gaps in the AWS interface and in the Amazon online store, where executable script code could be open to cross-site scripting attacks. Because of this major security issue and rather cumbersome sharing that inhibits collaboration, it turns out that Amazon Cloud is great for uploading photos and media files, etc. in order to free up space on your hard

The 4 Hour Work Week Tool Box

drive, but it's not recommended as a business-oriented platform.

The 4 Hour Work Week Tool Box

CHAPTER FIVE: EVERNOTE

Evernote is a note-taking app that syncs between your home computer, work computer, and smartphone and allows you to take notes in a variety of formats (typing, clip text from the web, voice, photo, etc.). Evernote can be installed as an independent program on a computer, an app on a smartphone, or simply run from any internet web browser. You create a free account at www.evernote.com and then create a unique login and password and start creating notes.

You can create and store pretty much any type of note you want to with Evernote. You can create a new note by typing text into the Evernote notepad (which is set up like a simplified version of Microsoft Word), record an audio note, take a picture of anything (post-it note, scraps of paper with handwritten notes on them, clippings from newspapers or magazines, etc.), or upload Microsoft Office documents like Word Documents, Excel spreadsheets, PowerPoints, etc. The cool thing is that you can take photo notes with your smartphone, which is **very** convenient. So, if you're the type of person that takes a lot of notes on post-its or scraps of paper and then loses them, go with Evernote. Take all those little scraps of paper and take photos with Evernote and throw the scraps away!

One other advantage of Evernote is that you can install the Evernote web clipper that you can install on any internet browser, making it extremely useful for clipping information out of web pages. It clips the text and/or photos on the web page, and then a window pops up with

The 4 Hour Work Week Tool Box

the information that you clipped pre-filled in a note, ready for you to title it and choose what folder to store it in.

You can arrange the notes in different notebooks all with easy-to-navigate drop down menus. Any time you create a new note, you'll choose which notebook you want to place it into. You can then make those notebooks either private–saved on your local computer–or shared across all of your devices, including work and home computers and your smartphone.

Another great thing about Evernote is that you can take notes by clipping from webpages using a web browser add-on (Mozilla, Chrome, or Safari). I use this function ALL the time whenever I'm doing any research online.

In the mobile devices' area, Evernote iPhone app really shines: it's really pretty user friendly, it's easy to scroll through your different notes, and it's pretty easy to search for notes.

A pretty slick add-on app that greatly improves the functionality of Evernote on your iPhone or iPad is EverClip. EverClip allows you to not only clip from web browsers on your smartphone but also allows you to clip from any app as well. This is extremely convenient on the iPhone or iPad because you can then clip from emails or from Notes or your calendar.

Evernote is 100% free. BUT, if you upgrade to the premium version for 5 bucks a month (or $45/year) you get a bunch of features, but two that are *just amazing:*

The 4 Hour Work Week Tool Box

1- The ability to let someone share your notebooks and vice versa, meaning you can access their notes, modify them, etc. GREAT for businesses, husbands and wives, etc.

2- The ability to passcode protect your account.

3- **You can search inside ANY document in any of your notebooks without opening up the document!** Take a photo of a newspaper clipping? You can find a phrase or word *in that newspaper clipping without opening it up and manually looking for the word or phrase.* Same goes for Word docs, PDF's, anything! **TRULY AMAZING.**

"One pretty useful way to utilize both Evernote and Google Drive together is to help manage your documents and data in your Evernote and Google Drive accounts and make sure you clean them out regularly. In Evernote, you can make a note with a reminder to clean out your old notes in both Evernote and Google Drive.

You might ask, "How do I know what to keep and what to delete?" Good question. I use this method, which works well and to date I've been able to avoid deleting anything truly important as well as minimizing clutter in my Google Drive and Evernote accounts: I go through and if I haven't accessed the note in the last 2 months, I open it and see if it's something that I foresee needing access to in the next 6 months. If yes, then I keep it. If not, away it goes! Try this method out and set these parameters to

The 4 Hour Work Week Tool Box

help keep your cloud storage programs neat, tidy, and uncluttered.

Chapter Six: Comparison of Cloud Storage Programs & Recommendations

Now, and after reviewing the four most popular cloud storage services, let's see how they compare to each other in terms of all the elements that matter to us as end users:

Ease of use: This is where Dropbox is unrivaled, featuring the start-up checklist which is a simple step-by-step explanation of all the service's features. In the same context, Google Drive offers a fairly smart intuitive interface but it's a bit more cumbersome than Dropbox. Evernote takes a bit more work to learn but once competent, you can fly through the program and Amazon Cloud is the least intuitive. As an aside, the ebook "Evernote Essentials" provides a comprehensive explanation of all features of Evernote, and I'd recommend it to get the most out of the program.

Free storage space: Google Drive provides 15 GB shared between Drive, Gmail, and Photos. Amazon Cloud is a bit less, offering 5 GB, in addition to the Cloud Player for media. This is far greater than the 2 GB offered by Dropbox, and the rather tiny monthly 60 MB allotment of Evernote.

Paid storage plans: Obviously, Amazon crushes the competition here; offering good plans beginning from $10 yearly. Google comes next; with monthly plans beginning from $2.49. Then comes Evernote; offering $5 monthly (or $45 yearly) plan. And Dropbox comes at last,

The 4 Hour Work Week Tool Box

with monthly plans beginning from $9.99 (or $99 yearly). But remember, this shouldn't be the sole criterion that determines which service to choose; services' features are the most important, and anyway, you might not even need more than the provided free space, as I've never gone over the monthly storage even on Evernote.

Ease of sharing: Dropbox provides quite a bit easier file sharing than Google Drive and Evernote, which take more keystrokes and clicks to share files. Also, Dropbox includes a variety of options for sharing, providing either read-only access or full read-and-write access, offered by Google Drive as well, which obviously enhances collaboration. Amazon Cloud offers sharing only via providing a link to the shared item which makes it the least useful for sharing and collaboration. Google Drive makes sharing documents easy especially if you have a Google account, but also adds the ability to share via Facebook and Twitter, although it's arguable whether you'd need that feature.

Photo sharing: In addition to sharing media files, this is where Amazon Cloud Drive outperforms, by offering special apps that allow you to back-up your iPhone photo galleries, and your shared albums become accessible from any iOS device. On the other hand, we find that Dropbox still needs to enhance photo sharing options. Also, Google Drive and Evernote are a bit more complex in terms of photo sharing but come in ahead of Dropbox.

Preview office documents: Both Google Drive and Evernote provide the ability to preview office documents, with the edge going to Google Drive, as when you open a file, it opens in Google Drive's own version of the relevant

The 4 Hour Work Week Tool Box

Office program. This allows you can manage files online without having to open up the office program, save the file, then re-upload it to the cloud, as you have to do with Evernote, where your files are stored as actual Office files. In this respect, Dropbox and Amazon Cloud Drive are completely out of competition as they don't provide options for previewing office documents.

Security: In addition to emailing you to seek verification prior to sharing or changing any of your data, Dropbox also provides even more security through the optional two-factor authentication, which helps largely eliminate many serious security gaps. A similar feature is provided by Google Drive (but you need to sign up for it (don't worry, its free)), and Evernote Premium has the additional PIN code lock. Clearly this is a point where Amazon Cloud largely falls short as they have no two factor verification which is becoming the standard base for security online.

The "X" Factor: There is one unique feature that is only available on Evernote Premium as I discussed above: the ability to search *within* PDF's, documents, and photos. I wouldn't base my choice on cloud storage programs only on this factor, but that feature is incredible in its own right and should be considered when choosing a cloud storage program.

So, what's the bottom line? Which one should I use? Obviously this depends on the file types intended for cloud storage, and what you need these files for. If you're just looking to store family photos, Amazon Cloud is the obvious choice, but if you need anything more than that you should look at the other 3 titans of cloud storage. As

The 4 Hour Work Week Tool Box

I've recommended extensively on Four Hour Physician, utilizing *any* sort of cloud storage program is going to simplify your life tremendously, as no longer will you need to shuffle through piles of papers to find what you need. In the end, I would recommend trying out all four programs and see what works best for you and makes the most sense for you. Give them all a try, and you'll be able to free your time and liberate your life!

One Final Note

I hope you've found this book interesting and informative. Please take a look at my other books, including, "Free Time: How To Hire A Virtual Assistant And Liberate Your Life" and my soon-to-be published "Little Book Of Contentment For Physicians". To contact me, please message me on Twitter, Facebook, or visit the Four Hour Physician website.

The 4 Hour Work Week Tool Box

Project Management Tools

For Everyday Life

Meg Smolinski & George Smolinski, M.D.

The 4 Hour Work Week Tool Box

TABLE OF CONTENTS

Introduction 74
Chapter One: Trello 77
Chapter Two: Nozbe 103
Chapter Three: Asana 120
Chapter Four: Comparison and Bottom Line 152
Disclaimer 162

The 4 Hour Work Week Tool Box

INTRODUCTION

In my daily routine, I have a habit that I picked up a while ago and now would never quit, because it helps me monitor my productivity level and bring my progress into focus. At the end of my day, I usually take a couple of minutes to sit quietly, disconnect from all my activities, close my eyes, and review everything I've done during the day. I see my day as a long series of small progress on big projects; it seems that my day usually consists of a wide range of activities related to my work in the clinic, tasks and projects related to my online business in addition to the personal and family-related activities.

With all these different tasks and activities in my daily routine, it frequently happens that when I review what I've done during a specific day, I find out that I've completely forgotten about some tasks that I should have done. I've tried it all including post-its, Google Tasks, Google Calendar events, and more. Obviously, this "oh crap I forgot to do 'X'" is a common problem that happens to almost everyone. Whether you're a business owner, an employee, or a student, whatever your career or your lifestyle, you suddenly remember something like the phone call that you should have made, the email message that you should have sent, or the important meeting that you should have attended during that day.

Going back to my own case, I'm a huge fan of hiring virtual assistants; that's no secret. With the team of virtual assistants that are helping manage my life, I'm always having to assign them to tasks and then follow up

The 4 Hour Work Week Tool Box

with their progress on the tasks they're working on. I also have VA team management activities that have to be integrated into my daily routine in addition to all the business tasks and personal activities that I'm doing.

What I finally realized is that managing such an incredibly crowded daily routine was overworking my mind! It's really laborious to be constantly concerned about remembering all the things that I should do, and there's always the fear that I might miss out on something important. So the big question was: Is there a better way to manage my day? Is there a better way to schedule all my activities and run my team of VAs?

"Well, yes there is." This was from my friend Jason Jordan who introduced me to Trello; the free task management app that allowed me to organize both my business-related tasks and my personal activities. Most importantly, it also enabled me to seamlessly manage my team of VAs.

In addition to Trello, there are several task management platforms available online, like Nozbe and Asana. Both Nozbe and Asana have been around for a while and have been getting a lot of great press along with Trello. When I reviewed the basic features of both Nozbe and Asana, I found that they are as efficient and useful as Trello but they each have unique qualities and characteristics that make them better (or worse) for certain types of people. Having researched the qualities and feature of Trello, Nozbe, and Asana, I felt it was important to share my findings and my knowledge with you as you no doubt have the same struggles I have with juggling many plates at once.

The 4 Hour Work Week Tool Box

In this book, I'll introduce you to the three program: Trello, Nozbe, and Asana, each in a separate chapter, giving a detailed explanation of the features in each program and how to use it. And the last chapter in this book I have an itemized comparison of the three apps, where you can see clearly their relative strengths and weaknesses.

By introducing this book to you, I'm conveying my experience about Trello, Nozbe, and Asana in an unbiased review, so that you can make a thoughtful decision on which task management platform is the best to use. However, whatever the platform that you choose, I have no doubt that using any of these project management platforms will improve the workflow of your business, enhance your productivity and help you make the most of your time.

Now, before we get started, a few tips about using this book. First, I'd highly recommend reading this book as a tab in your web browser using the Kindle app for your web browser, which is free and can be found here.

Second, the best way to decide which tool to use is to actually USE it, so I'd also recommend setting up a free account with each of these programs as I take you through them in the book. There are links to each program in the book, and again the only way to decide which one is best for you is to get in there, get dirty, and take a hard look at which one is the best for *you*.

Let's get started!

Chapter One: Trello

Trello is a really efficient task management tool, it's easy to use, and it's the tool that I'm actually using to manage the tasks I assign to my VAs, and manage some of the work in my clinic as well.

The main reason why Trello is a great task management program is that it's very streamlined and user-friendly, and it is easy for new users to explore its features and get up to speed right away. In this chapter, I'll walk you through the main features of the app, explaining in detail how to use Trello to build and manage your task management system.

To start using Trello, go to www.trello.com and sign up for a free account. You can go through the traditional sign up process by putting in a name, email, and password, or you can sign up with your Google account which is strongly recommended--I'll point out later in this chapter the reason why it's so good to sign up with Trello using your Google account.

The Task Management Structure

In Trello, the basic task management structure consists of the following positions:

The Organization (optional) is a workspace, or a broad category of projects. The Organization consists of a group of Boards (projects). As you see below, the Organization is an optional position; you can either create Boards (projects) within Organizations, or set up individual Boards that don't come within Organizations.

The 4 Hour Work Week Tool Box

· **The Board** is actually a project, and it consists of a group of Lists. The default setting under each Board (i.e. project) is "To Do", "Doing", and "Done". These lists can be easily re-labeled and you can add more lists if you desire.

· **The List** ("To Do", "Doing", and "Done") consists of a group of Cards.

· **The Card** represents a task. In the Card, you actually include all the resources and actions that you need to get the task done, along with the assignee, which is the person who is responsible for accomplishing the task. The Card is the basic unit of work in Trello, and I'll cover Cards in detail later on.

Now, this is how to put this structure into action: when you open your Trello account for the first time, the generic Welcome Board (depicted below) will be your starting point to start building your task management system. As you see in the screenshot, clicking on "New Board" opens up a window where you choose whether to create a new Board or a new Organization, and to give a title to the new Board/Organization that will be created.

The 4 Hour Work Week Tool Box

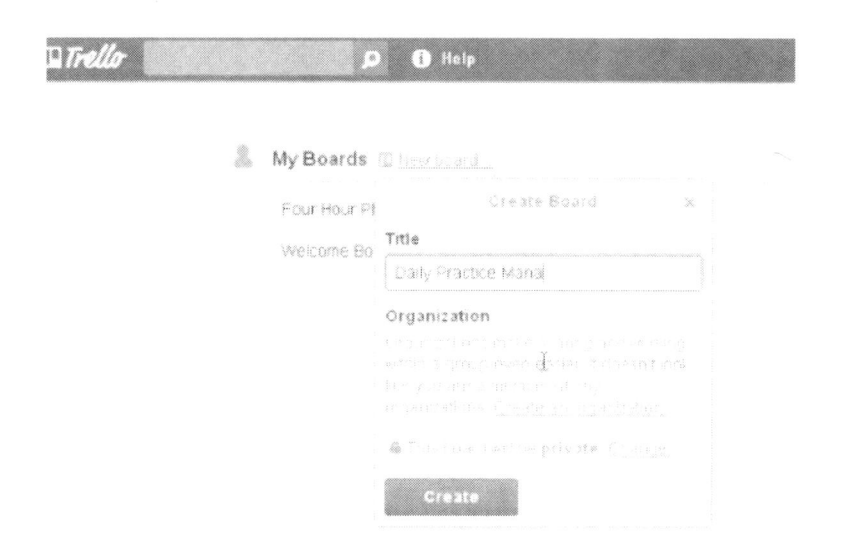

In Trello, you can create as many Organizations, Boards, Lists, and Cards as you want. But as an example here, let's say that when you start setting up your task management structure, you'll begin with creating two Organizations, and you call one of them "Business," and call the other one "Personal." Having these two Organizations set up, you'll then start adding Boards to them; create a new Board under the "Business" Organization for every business-related project/event, and create a new Board under the "Personal" Organization for every personal or family-related project/event.

The Board is the unit in the task management structure under which every List and Card will fall, and the upcoming part of the chapter demonstrates how to manage the Trello Boards, how to create tasks within the Boards, how to invite people to become Board members, and how to assign these members to the tasks within the Board.

The 4 Hour Work Week Tool Box

The Board

The screenshot below depicts a typical Trello Board. As you see in the screenshot, the Board is entitled "Four Hour Physician," and includes the three default Lists that come with any newly created Board in Trello. As their names imply, the default Board Lists are:

- **To Do List**, where you add Trello Cards for the tasks that you're planning to do.

- **Doing List**, where you add Trello Cards for the tasks that you're currently doing.

- **Done List**, where you put the Trello Cards that you have completed.

After creating a new Board, and as long as the Lists within that Board are still empty, each of these Lists has an "Add a card" button that you can see in the screenshot below--it appears in the center "Doing" list. Clicking on that button allows you to add the first Card to the current List. And when there is at least one Card on a specific List, a green "Add" button appears on that List, and allows you to add new Cards to it. You can see this button in the "To Do" List depicted in the below screenshot. After you have added a number of Cards within a specific List, you can rearrange those Cards inside the List by clicking, dragging and dropping the Cards. You can use this feature to prioritize Cards; put the Card that holds the most important task at the top of the List, and order the Cards all the way down to the Card that holds the least important task at the bottom of the List.

The 4 Hour Work Week Tool Box

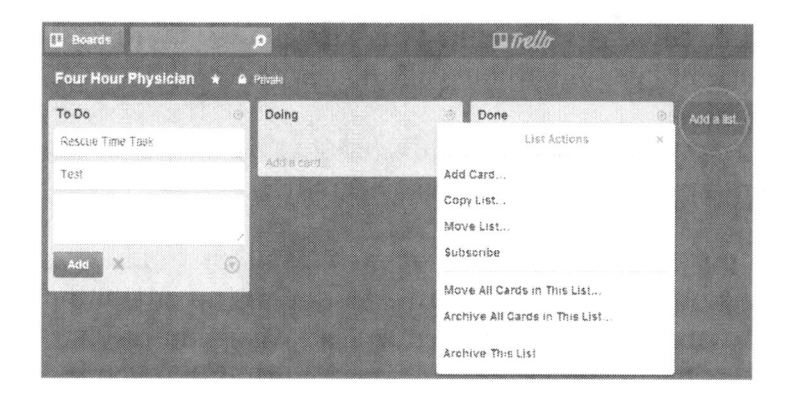

List Actions

Each list has a down arrow that appears next to its title. Clicking on that down arrow opens up the menu (depicted above) that includes the following List actions:

• **Add Card** allows you to add new Cards to the current List.

• **Copy List** allows you use the current List as a template; to create a copy of the current List that includes a copy of all the Cards within the initial List.

• **Move List** allows you to change the location of the List and put it in another Board, or change its position in the current Board.

• **Subscribe** allows you to be notified of every new activity that happens within the List.

• **Move All Cards in List** allows you to move all the Cards in the current List to another List in the current Board.

The 4 Hour Work Week Tool Box

- **Archive All Cards in This List** allows you to keep the current List and archive all the Cards within it.

- **Archive This List** allows you to archive the current List with all the Cards within it.

It's important to note here that each List is customizable; clicking on the title of a specific List opens up an editing field where you can rename that List. Also, you can add new lists by clicking the "Add a List" button that you see in the red circle in the above screenshot. You can add as many Lists as you want and give them the titles that match your task management style.

The screenshot above depicts an example of a Trello Board used to manage a specific project, and that Board has been customized to match that type of project. In this example, unlike the default Board settings, the Board includes four Lists, and these Lists are holding the titles "Ideas," "Pitch," "Approved," and "Implementation," respectively. Actually, the ability to customize Trello Lists is a pretty slick feature that makes Trello a robust choice for planning projects of any kind.

The 4 Hour Work Week Tool Box

Managing Boards

Trello Boards are managed through two parts in the app: the top toolbar, and the right pane of Trello screen. You can see both parts in the screenshot below.

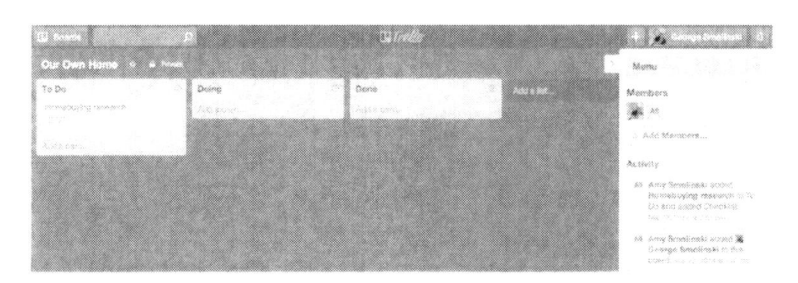

The top toolbar includes the following features:

The Boards button opens up a list that includes all your Boards and Organizations. This list also includes a search field where you can search for a particular Board by name.

The search field is where you can search for particular Cards using the Card name.

Clicking on the "Trello" button at the center gives you an overall view of all your Boards and Organizations.

The plus button on the right hand side allows you to create a new Board or a new Organization.

Clicking on the bell symbol shows you notifications of all the activities that occur in all the Cards that you're contributing to. If the bell appears red, then you have new notifications pending; if it's blue, then there are no new notifications.

The 4 Hour Work Week Tool Box

Clicking on the button that has your name and avatar on it opens up a list that includes the following items:

- Profile: Allows you to edit your profile.

- Cards: Displays all the Cards that you're contributing to.

- Settings: Allows you to edit your account details.

- Apps: Allows you to download Trello apps for mobile devices.

- Share Trello: Gives you a link that you can share with other people to invite them to join Trello.

- Help: That's where you can search for anything you want to know about how to use Trello.

The Right Pane

As depicted in the screenshot above, the right pane includes three sections: "Menu," "Members," and "Activity." The screenshot below depicts the "Menu."

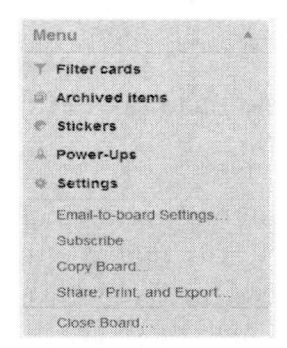

```
Menu
  Filter cards
  Archived items
  Stickers
  Power-Ups
  Settings
     Email-to-board Settings...
     Subscribe
     Copy Board...
     Share, Print, and Export...
     Close Board...
```

84

The 4 Hour Work Week Tool Box

The Menu includes the following features:

Filter Cards allows you to filter cards according to the label, members, and/or due date.

Stickers are emoticons and similar stickers (like you see in Facebook Messaging) that you can add to your cards

Archived items feature allows you to retrieve archived Cards.

Settings include the following actions:

- *Rename Board*

- *Change Organization* allows you to move the Board from its current Organization to another Organization.

- *Change visibility* allows you to determine who can see and edit the Board items. There are three levels of Board visibility in Trello:

- Private: When you set a particular Board to be private, only you and the people you add as Board members will be able to view and edit the items within that Board.

- Organizations: Means that the Board will be visible only to the members of the Organization to which that Board belongs. But editing the Board items will be open only for the Board members.

- Public: The public Board is visible to anyone that has the link to that Board. Also, the public Board shows up in search engines like Google, but editing the Board items is open only for the Board members.

· **Commenting permissions** allows you to determine, for a specific Board, who can leave comments inside the Cards within that Board. There are five levels of commenting permission:

·   Disabled: No one is allowed to comment.

·   Members: Admins and normal members only are allowed to comment (the terms "Admin," "Normal Member," and "Observer" will be explained in this chapter in "Permissions").

·   Members and Observers (available only for Trello Business Class account owners): allows admins, normal members, and observers to comment.

·   Organization members: allows admins, normal members, observers, and Organization members to comment.

·   Public members: allows any Trello member to comment.

· **Invitation permissions** allows you to determine who is able to invite people to the current Board. There are two options for invitation permissions:

·   Admins: allows only admins to invite people to join the Board.

·   All members: allows both members and admins to invite people to join the Board.

The 4 Hour Work Week Tool Box

· ***Allow Organization members to join:*** any Organization member can join this Board without receiving an invitation. To enable this feature, the Board setting for "Change Visibility" – explained above – must be either "Organization" or "Public," it can't be "Private."

· ***Edit label names*** allows you to edit the names of the color labels that you can use to tag specific Cards within the current Board. This color coding feature will be explained shortly.

Back at the "Menu," the remaining items are:

Email-to-Board settings gives you a unique email address that you can use to add Cards to the current Board (later in this chapter you'll see in detail how to send Cards via email). Also, "Email-to-Board Settings" include the following actions:

· <u>Generate a new email address</u> generates another email address in case you want to replace the current email address that you're using to send Cards to the current Board. If you click on "Generate a new email address," the old email will be terminated permanently.

· <u>Email me this address:</u> Having got the email address that you'll use to send Cards to the current Board, this feature sends that email address to your email inbox, so that you can seamlessly add it to your contact list.

· <u>Your emailed Cards appear in</u> allows you to choose the List and position in the List where the emailed Cards will be added.

The 4 Hour Work Week Tool Box

Subscribe: when you subscribe to a Board, you'll be notified of every new activity made in any Card within that Board.

Copy Board: allows you to use the current Board as a template.

Share, Print, and Export: allows you to print the current Board, gives you a link that you can share with other people so that they can join the current Board, and "Export" stands for opening the current Board in the JavaScript Object Notation form.

Close Board: archives the current Board, and if you want to re-open a closed Board, click on the "Boards" button in the top toolbar, select "View Closed Boards," find the one that you want, and click "Re-open".

Members

As you can see in the screenshot below, the "Members" feature lies in the right pane underneath "Menu". "Members" is the place where you can see all the people that are joining the Board. Clicking on the "Add Members" button that you see in the screenshot opens up a search field where you can search for people on Trello in order to invite them to join the current Board. When an invitee accepts your invitation, they will become a Board member, and their avatar will show up on the right pane, as you see in the screenshot.

The 4 Hour Work Week Tool Box

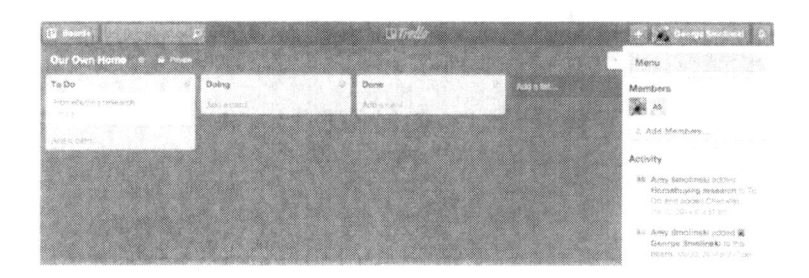

Activity

This is the section that includes all the activities that take place within the current Board. Every new activity comes at the top of that list in chronological order with the newest activities at the top of the list.

Working Within a Board on Trello

The Card

The Card is the place where you put a task or tasks that you want to work on

Managing Cards:

Card Actions

When you hover with your mouse cursor on a Card, you'll see a dropdown arrow. Clicking on that arrow opens up the "Card Actions" menu, shown below.

The 4 Hour Work Week Tool Box

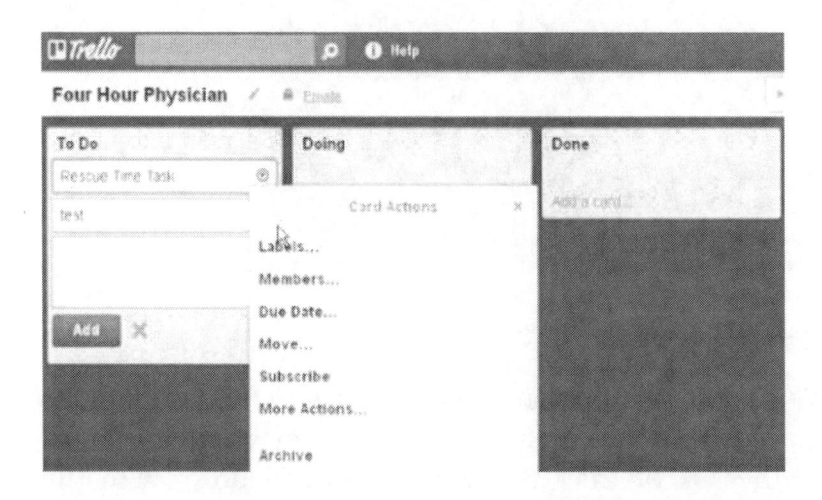

The "Card Actions" menu includes the following actions:

•   The Labels feature allows you to add a color label to the Card. It also allows you to edit the titles of the color labels. This is actually one of the features that I really enjoy in Trello. I'm a visual guy so the color codes help me manage projects a bit better.

•   The Members feature allows you to invite one or more members of the current Board to join the Card. The same thing can be done by using the Board members' avatars. As you see in the screenshot below, the Board members' avatars are located in the right pane of the screen. If you want to add a Board member to a specific Card, you can simply drag that person's avatar from the right pane and drop it into that Card.

The 4 Hour Work Week Tool Box

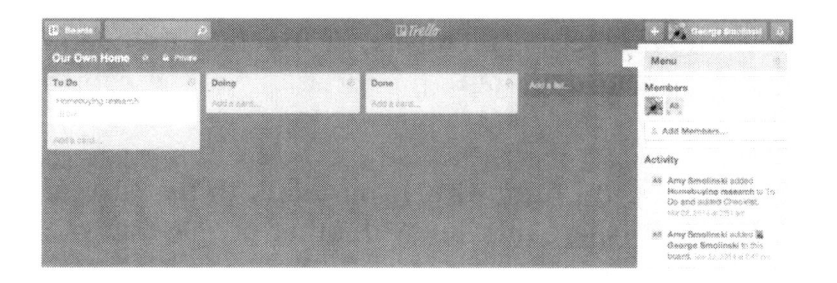

- Due date allows you to add a due date for the Card.

- Move allows you to move the Card to another Board, or to move the Card to the top, middle, or bottom of another List inside the same Board.

- Subscribe: When you subscribe to a specific Card, you'll be notified of every new activity that occurs on that Card.

- Archive is where you put the completed Cards.

- More Actions include the following features:

- Attach File: Allows you to add files from your Computer, Dropbox, Box, and OneDrive account. It also allows you to drag and drop files and links into the Card. The notable thing here is that if you use your Google account when you sign up with Trello - which is preferable, as I mentioned in the beginning of this chapter - you'll be able to import items into Trello Cards directly from your Google Drive.

- Copy: Allows you to use the current Card as a template, create a copy of it, add a title to that copy, choose which items to keep from the original Card

The 4 Hour Work Week Tool Box

(checklists, labels, members, attachments, and comments), and determine the location for the copied Card.

• *Link to this Card*: Gives you a link to the current Card. You can share this link with other people that you want to invite to join that Card.

The Card Status Window

Clicking on a Card within a List opens up the window, shown below, that includes the Card status and actions.

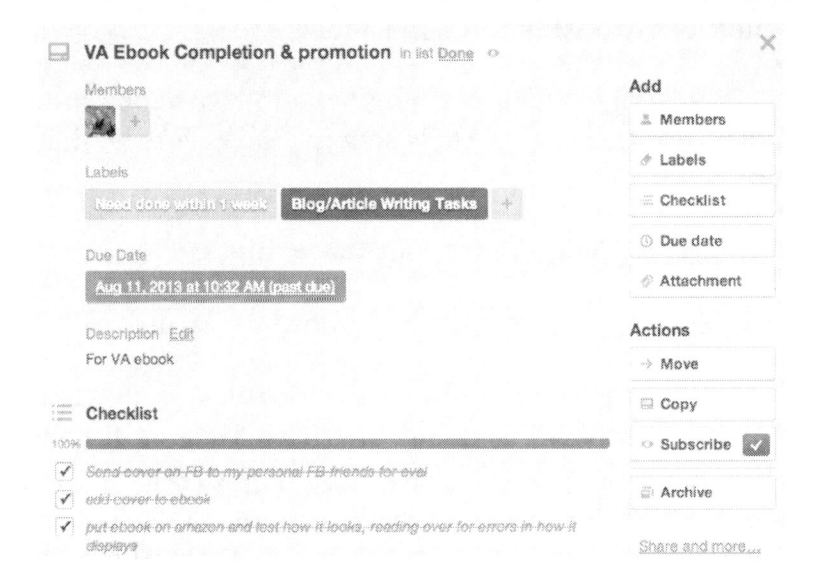

In the above screenshot, the right pane of the Card status window lists Card actions. These actions are divided into two categories:

• **Add:** includes "Members," "Labels," "Due date," and "Attachment," which are the same functions that you saw in "Card Actions" menu, besides a "Checklist" function that allows you to add a checklist to the Card, add a title to that checklist, and make a copy of that checklist in another Card.

• **Actions:** includes "Move," "Subscribe," "Archive," "Copy," "Link to this Card," and "Share and More." This last feature includes a link to the Card, the number of the Card, and the "Export JSON" feature that opens the Card in the JavaScript Object Notation form.

Also in the above-depicted Card status window, the left pane shows all the settings and items within the Card. At the top of the left pane, you can see the Card name and the List to which that Card belongs. Also, you can see the Board members who are joining the Card, the color label (the plus sign beside the color label allows you to add more than one color label to the Card), the due date of the Card, and the Card items such as checklists and attachments. As you see above, the Card has a checklist, and the great thing about the checklist is that when one of the Card members completes an item, they click inside that item's checkbox in order to cross it out. This is very useful for you as it allows you to keep track of the progress on the Card just by taking a look at the checklist and seeing how many items are crossed out. Additionally, Trello automatically saves each checklist as a template, and by clicking on the "Checklist" button on the right hand side of the card, your previous checklists will appear and you can import them with a click of the mouse. This is fantastic for repetitious tasks!

The 4 Hour Work Week Tool Box

Email Cards to Trello

As I pointed out earlier in this chapter, you can email Cards to the Trello Board by using a Board-specific email address. In order to get that email address, go to the right pane of the Trello screen that you see in the screenshot below.

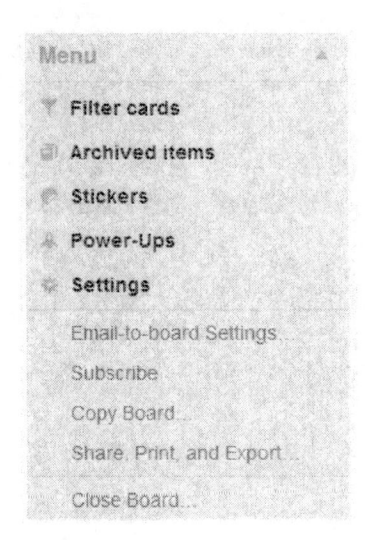

Menu
- Filter cards
- Archived items
- Stickers
- Power-Ups
- Settings
- Email-to-board Settings
- Subscribe
- Copy Board
- Share, Print, and Export
- Close Board

Within the right pane, open the "Menu," and choose "Email-to-Board settings," and the window, shown below, will appear.

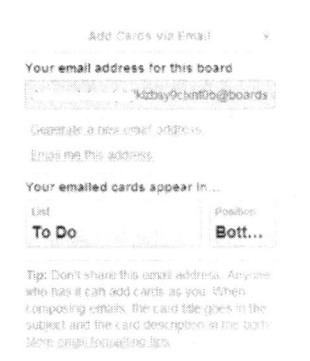

The 4 Hour Work Week Tool Box

As you see in the above screenshot, this window shows the unique email address for the current Board. Shown also is the customizable location where the emailed Cards will be added within the current Board. As you see above, the default location setting is the bottom of the "To Do" list. The screenshot below depicts a typical Card being sent via email.

The email above will translate into the following:

·   The subject of the email will be the title of the Card.

·   The body of the email will be the description of the Card.

·   The color label is added within the subject line. As you see above, the color label is represented by the hashtag sign followed by the color label's name or color, which is the case here: "#red"

The 4 Hour Work Week Tool Box

- The "@" sign in the subject line is followed by the Board member's name – "Emma" in this example – that will be added to the Card.

- If you need to attach items to the Card, you can attach these items to the email.

Now, the screenshot below depicts the Card after it has been emailed to the Board.

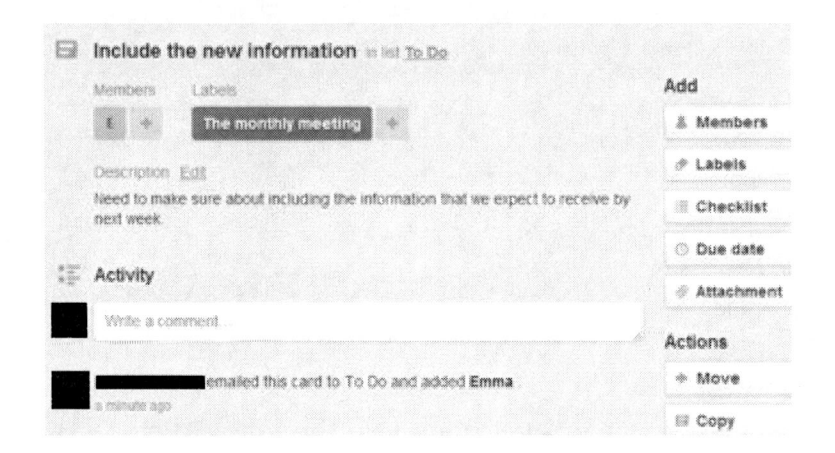

The screenshot above depicts the Card status window of the emailed Card. As you can see, the Card title is at the top, the avatar of the added Board member appears under "Members" that you see on the left hand side, the color label is applied, and the Card description is included just as in the email.

One thing to note here is that if the Card has attachments, the size of the attachments cannot exceed 10 MB in order for the Card to be created.

The 4 Hour Work Week Tool Box

Permissions within the Board

For any Board member, the permissions of the Board member are the privileges given to them on the actions that they can do within the Board. In order to specify the permissions of Board members, head over to the right pane of the screen shown below, where you can see the avatars that represent all the Board members.

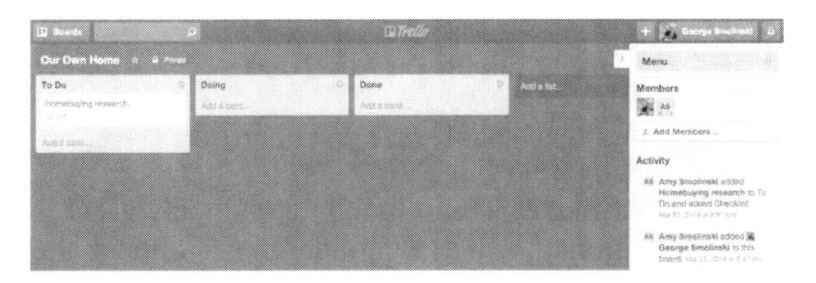

Clicking on the avatar of a Board member opens up a window where you can specify their privileges on the Board. There are three types of member permissions:

·   Admin: The admin can view and comment on Cards, remove Board members, and change the settings of the Board. The notable thing here is that the Board can have more than one admin.

·   Normal: The normal member can view and comment on Cards, but cannot change Board settings.

·   Observer: The observer member (in Trello Business Class only) can view and comment on Cards within the Board, but cannot move or edit Cards or changes Board settings.

The 4 Hour Work Week Tool Box

Trello for mobile

Besides the web-based app, Trello provides native apps for the following mobile devices:

- iPhone and iPad (iOS 7+); available on iTunes.

- Android phones and tablets (4+) available on Google Play.

- Kindle Fire; available on Amazon

- Windows 8; available on apps.microsoft.com

The thing that makes Trello mobile apps really great is that the functionality of the mobile app is almost the same as the functionality of the web-based app. Also, the mobile app is very user-friendly and easy to navigate, which makes it a very useful tool that allows you to access and manage all your Trello Boards and Cards on the go.

Just like the web-based app, in order to open the Trello mobile app, you can either login with your Google account, or with the email-password authentication.

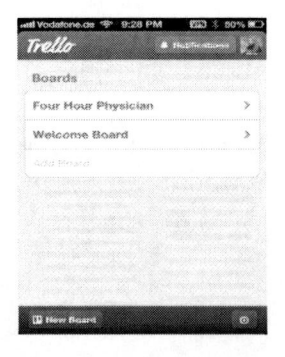

The 4 Hour Work Week Tool Box

The screenshot above depicts the first screen that comes up when you log into Trello from your mobile. This screen features the Trello Boards, as well as the notification button that, when clicked, brings up notifications of the new activities that occur within all the Trello Boards that you're subscribing to. And if you want to add new Boards, you can click on the "New Board" button that you see at the bottom of the screenshot above.

Now, you can open any Board and manage Lists and Cards within it. As an example, I'll click on the Four Hour Physician Board that you can see above, and this will open up a screen where you can see the Lists within that Board.

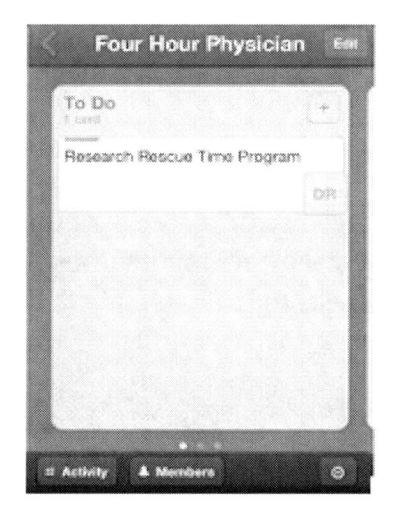

The above screenshot depicts the "To Do" List within the Four Hour Physician Board. As you see above, this List includes a Card named "Research Rescue Time Program." Also, you can see the color label of the Card, and the box in the bottom right corner of the Card is the place where

99

The 4 Hour Work Week Tool Box

you see the initials of the member to whom this Card is assigned.

Obviously, the app shows one List at a time, and allows you to slide seamlessly through the different Lists within the Board. Also, you can change the location of any Card by dragging and dropping; you can change the Card's position within the List, or move the Card across Lists within the Board.

At the top right of the above screenshot, you'll also see a plus button which, when tapped, allows you to create a new Card within the current List. There is also the "Activity" button that you see at the bottom of the screen, which allows you to see all the activities that happen within your Boards. The "Members" button shows all the Board members, and allows you to seamlessly assign them to Cards within that Board.

Pricing plans

Obviously, you can get by very well with a free account on Trello, as long as the size of Card attachments doesn't exceed 10 MB, which would be enough if you need to attach Microsoft Office documents, PDF documents, and image files. But if you need to attach large size files such as videos, audio files, or Photoshop documents, you'll need to upgrade your Trello account to Trello Gold.

Trello Gold

With Trello Gold, you can have Card attachments of up to 250 MB size. Trello Gold is available at a monthly payment of $5, or a yearly payment $45. But you can enjoy Trello Gold for free for up to 13 months, and here is how.

When you upgrade your free account to Trello Gold, you will enjoy a month of Trello Gold for free. Moreover, you can invite people to join Trello and you'll be given a free month of Trello Gold for every person that you get to join Trello, up to 12 people. That means you can enjoy up to 12 months of using Trello Gold for free, in addition to the free month that you'll have once you upgrade your free account to Trello Gold, that's a total of 13 month of Trello Gold for free.

And in order to invite people to join Trello, you can use a link that Trello provides for this purpose. To get that link, go to the top toolbar, shown previously in this chapter, and click on the button that has your name and avatar on it. That button opens up a menu that includes "Share Trello," and there you can find the link that you can copy and share, post on Twitter and Facebook, and/or email to other people so that you get them to join Trello.

Business Class

If you're running teamwork projects and you need to have some advanced administrative features. You can use "Business Class." Each Trello Organization can be upgraded to Business Class at a monthly payment of $5 per user, or a yearly payment of $45 per user.

When you upgrade to Business Class, you're not going to upgrade the whole Trello account, but you're only going to upgrade certain Organizations within your account.

The 4 Hour Work Week Tool Box

The screenshot below depicts a typical Trello Organization, and the button that shows up on the right hand side allows you to upgrade this Organization to Business Class.

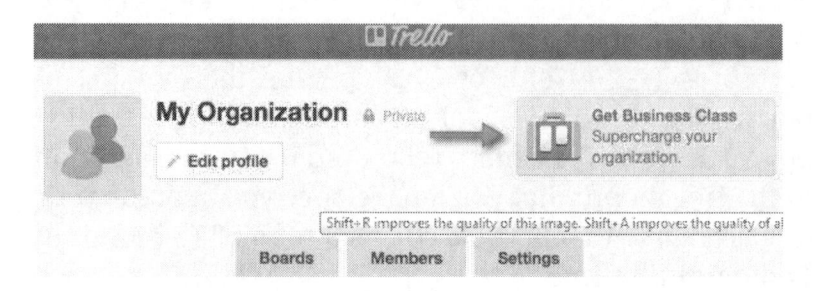

When you upgrade an Organization to Business class, you can enjoy having business-grade administrative features, enhanced security for your data, data proprietary levels so that you can determine which data will be visible to every member of your team, as well as getting your team to collaborate seamlessly on your teamwork business.

In summary, Trello is a very easy-to-use, powerful, and free platform for project management. Its very fast to learn, and if you want to see it in action, I've even recorded a free How-To-Use-Trello video that takes you through the entire setup process and shows you the tricks I've learned to get the most out of Trello.

CHAPTER TWO: NOZBE

Nozbe is another big player in the task management platform world. It has been around for a while and has been getting a lot of great press and for good reason: it's easy to use and works as well as my personal favorite, Trello.

In order to use Nozbe, go to www.nozbe.com and sign up for a free account; put in your name, email address, and the password, and you'll have your account created. As you'll see later in this chapter, the free Nozbe account allows you to have up to five open projects/contexts at a time.

The first notable thing about Nozbe is that the interface is intelligently organized. There is a menu on the left-- let's call it the main menu--listing all the partitions in your Nozbe account, a top toolbar, and a bottom toolbar. When you click on a certain partition in the main menu, these toolbars bring up the functions that you need for that partition. The screenshot below depicts these partitions and menus. This screenshot is going to be your reference as you read this chapter and see the basic features of Nozbe.

The 4 Hour Work Week Tool Box

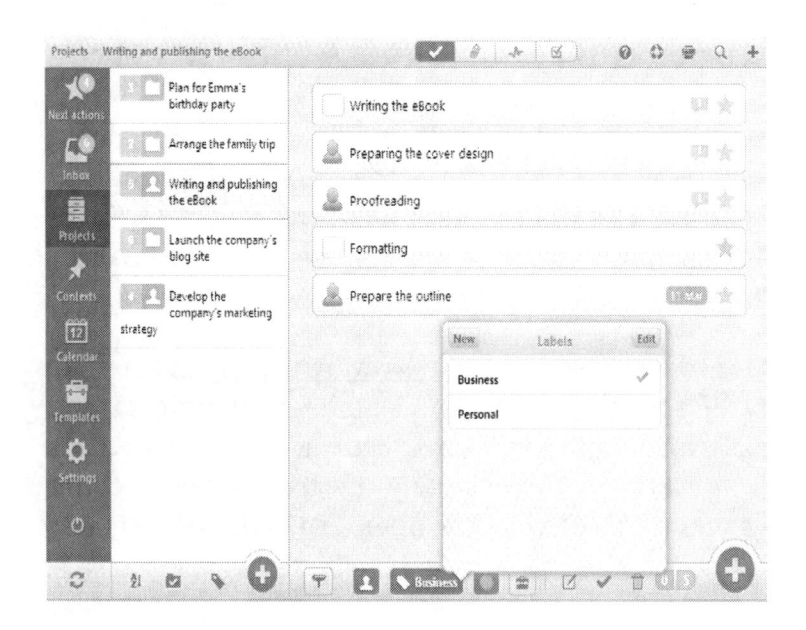

Projects

To create a new project, click on the "Projects" tab in the main menu, and then the bottom toolbar

The Bottom Toolbar

I'm first going to cover the bottom toolbar, as that's where you'll be doing the majority of your work within the Nozbe platform. The screenshot below depicts the bottom toolbar that appears upon clicking "Projects" in the main menu. Click on the red-circled plus sign to create a new project, and you'll be prompted to name the project, and then you'll be prompted to add tasks to that project.

The 4 Hour Work Week Tool Box

Now that you have some existing projects and tasks under them, let's see how to manage them using the various functions in the bottom toolbar.

Labels

For better arrangement and planning of your activities, it makes sense to have some projects grouped together so that you'll be able to see only one group of projects at a time; that's what the "Labels" feature allows you to do. As you can see in the first and second screenshots, there is a big "Labels" button in the middle of the bottom of the screen. To create a new label, click on the label button; this opens up a window where you can create new labels, edit existing ones, and change the label in certain projects, and you can also add a project to more than one label. Here, as an example, I made "Personal" and "Business" labels and the latter one appears on the label button because it's the label to which the currently opened project belongs.

Project Color Codes

Nozbe provides color-coding for the projects which is a feature that, as I mentioned earlier in the previous chapter, I use in Trello and really enjoy. To add a color code to a project, click on the button with the green circle that you see in the above screenshot, right in the middle of the bottom toolbar. Clicking that button opens up a list of colors to choose from. As an example here, I chose the green color for the current project.

The 4 Hour Work Week Tool Box

People In Project

If you need to invite people to collaborate with you on a project, click the button with the human head and shoulder symbol. Clicking that button opens up a window where you'll be prompted to provide the email addresses for your invitees, and then Nozbe emails them with a link that directs them to access the project.

Project Templates

Some of the activities we do in our life are habitual, done frequently, or always done in the same way. Preparing a shopping list, writing a blog post, or arranging for a weekend vacation are examples of recurrent activities that are mainly based on setting up a list of things, and this list remains the same except for some minor task-specific details that need to be changed when you prepare for these activities. Instead of creating a new project with similar tasks every time, Nozbe provides a "Project Templates" feature that allows you to create a project, fill it up with the specific tasks to be accomplished, and click on "Create Template" button (the one next to "Project Color" button in the bottom toolbar). After saving the project as a template, it appears in your "Template" list in the main menu, which you can see in the screenshot below. So, whenever you need to create a similar project, click on "Templates," get the needed project template, and you can then create a new project based on it.

The 4 Hour Work Week Tool Box

That covers the main functions of the bottom toolbar; here are the rest of the main functions in the bottom toolbar:

The pen and paper button allows you to rename an existing project.

When you complete a project, click on **the check mark button** to move that project from open projects to completed projects.

The folder with the check mark allows you to view your completed projects.

The plus sign button on the right hand side allows you to add tasks to existing projects. The same function is invoked by striking the "A" key on your keyboard.

The funnel button applies a filter for the current view. Clicking it allows you to choose the filtering criteria; you can see tasks having the same people, context, time, etc.

The 4 Hour Work Week Tool Box

Working Within A Project On Nozbe

Clicking on **Tasks** inside a project opens up a window containing the status of that task. The screenshot below depicts that status window on the right hand side of the screenshot. Click on the task's name and you'll be allowed to edit it. If you click the star at the top right of the status window, this task will be added to your "Next Actions" list (I'll talk more about "Next Actions" shortly). Under the task name, there are several tabs that represent task's parameters; the tab right under the task name represents the location of the task. Clicking that tab opens up a list--you can see it in the screenshot below--where you're allowed to change the location of the task and put it in another project or in the inbox if you need to. And if you click on the red button circled "New" you can create a new project for that task. The next tab in the task status window determines the person who is responsible for doing this task if the task belongs to a teamwork project.

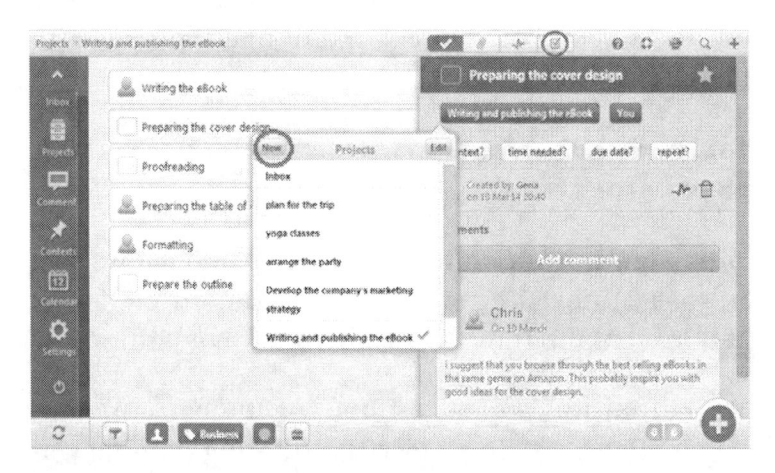

Here are the functions of the other tabs:

108

The 4 Hour Work Week Tool Box

Context defines the physical place where this task should be done. Default contexts are "Home," "Computer," and "Errands."

Time needed specifies a time period for tasks that need to be done, ranging from 5 minutes to 8 hours.

Due date specifies a date and time when you need the task done. It shows up in your Nozbe calendar in the main menu.

Repeat is for tasks that you need to do recurrently. You can set the task to be redone periodically such as every day, every weekday, every month, half a year, or every year. "Repeat" tasks are automatically starred and put in the "Next Actions" section, which I'll mention later in this chapter.

Add comment is the way Nozbe provides a variety of options for including necessary details and attaching files and notes related to tasks. You can type in text comments, type in a URL, attach files from your computer, add a checklist, put in an Evernote note, and upload an item from your Dropbox account.

Clicking inside the checkbox at the top left of the status window allows you to move that task from open tasks to completed tasks when a task is done. It remains there until midnight of the day it was moved and with the beginning of the next day, that task will be archived. If you find that a particular completed task needs further work, you'll see later in this chapter (in the top toolbar functions) how to reopen a completed task – provided that you do this before midnight of the day you checked

The 4 Hour Work Week Tool Box

it as completed! *This is a pretty important point, so be sure you understand the time limit on archiving tasks!*

Let's go back to the main menu and review the features included there.

Inbox

Some activities are of the types that don't need a list of things or procedures that need to be followed. Scheduling a yoga class or a dental exam are examples of this type of activity, and all you need your task management platform to do is to schedule standalone tasks for them. This is what Nozbe provides in the Inbox, where you can add individual tasks and, as needed, add all the details you need for those tasks as you've seen earlier in this chapter.

Adding a task to the Inbox can be done in four ways:

·   Through email

·   From your internet browser

·   From your Twitter account (these three methods will be explained in "Settings" below)

·   From the plus sign on the top right of Nozbe screen – it also allows adding tasks to existing projects – and here is how:

Clicking the plus sign – or pressing the "T" key on your keyboard – opens up a field (see the screenshot below) where you type in the name of the task and the hashtag after it. Doing this opens up a menu where you can

The 4 Hour Work Week Tool Box

specify all the parameters for that new task: where it will be added (the inbox or a certain project), the context where it should be handled, the person who will be responsible for it, the time period or date when it needs to be done, and if it's a reoccurring task, the time period when it needs to be repeated. And if you put it as a "Priority," this task will automatically be starred and put in your "Next Actions" section.

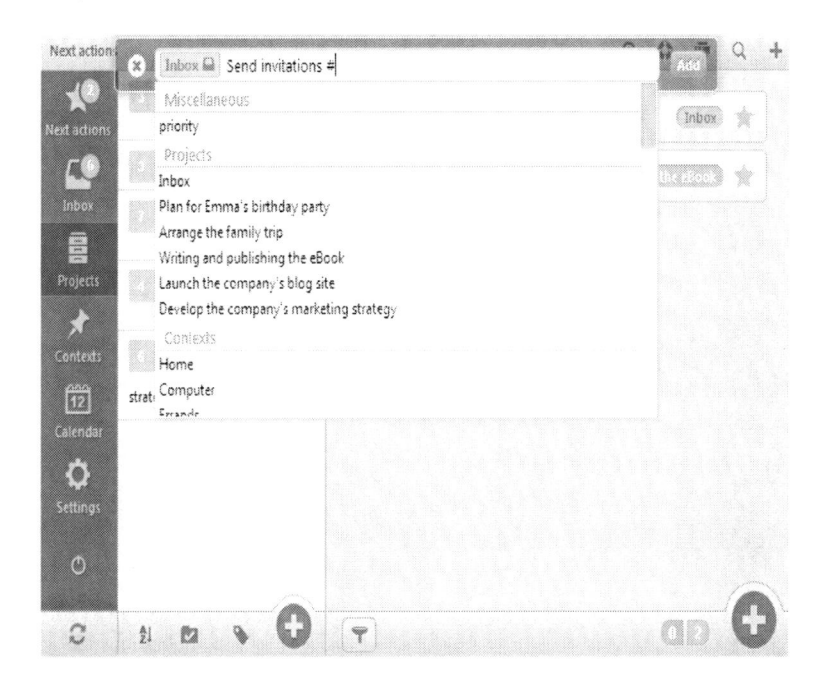

Next Actions

"Next Actions" is the reminder for your important tasks, and it's the first thing you see every time you log into your Nozbe account. Tasks scheduled as next actions are:

• Tasks for which you click the star next to their names in the task status window.

111

The 4 Hour Work Week Tool Box

- Tasks that are scheduled as recurring are automatically added to next actions.

Contexts

Clicking "Contexts" in the main menu opens up a list containing contexts such as "Home," "Computer," and "Errand." Click a particular context and you'll see all the tasks that you assigned to that context.

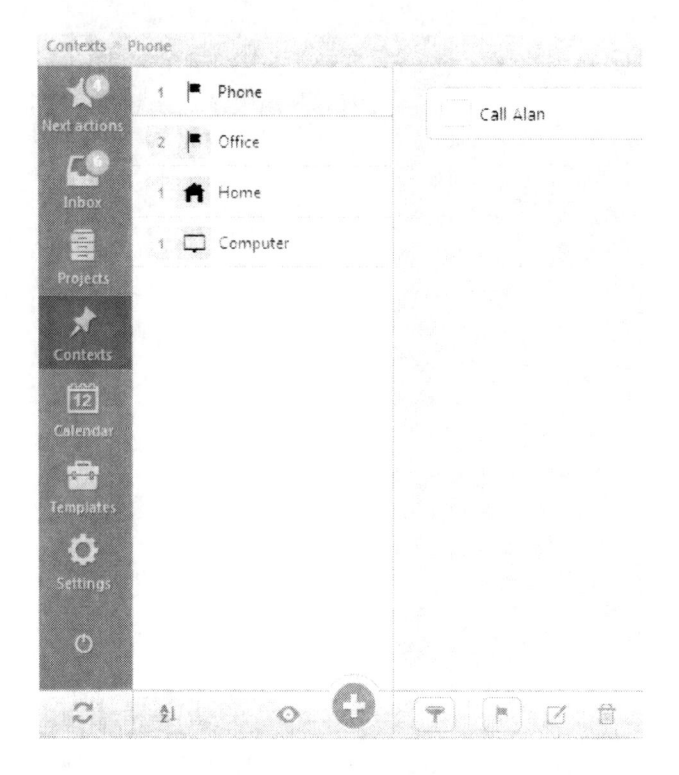

The screenshot above depicts what appears to you when you click "Contexts" in the main menu. If you're using the free plan, you can have up to 5 contexts and you can have those contexts tailored to fit your needs; you can add a new context by clicking the plus sign that you see at the

112

The 4 Hour Work Week Tool Box

bottom, and you can delete a context by clicking the trash can symbol at the bottom right of the screenshot. As an example here, I deleted some default contexts that I don't need, and added "Office" and "Phone" contexts instead.

Settings

Besides your personal info, "Settings" also includes tools that you can use to add tasks to your Nozbe inbox from your email, web browser, and your Twitter account. The screenshot below shows what appears to you when you click "Settings" in the main menu.

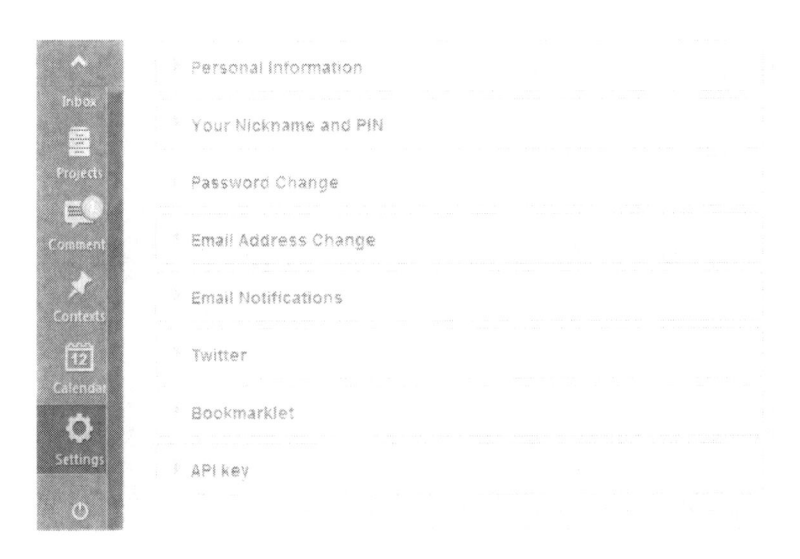

- **To add tasks from your web browser**, click on "Bookmarklet" and you'll find a link named "Add Action to Nozbe." You can simply drag that link and add it to your Favorites/Bookmarks. When you click it in your browser, you'll be prompted to type in a task name and

113

The 4 Hour Work Week Tool Box

then click on "Add Action to Nozbe" button, and the new task will be added to your Nozbe inbox.

· **To send messages from Twitter to Nozbe inbox**, go to your Twitter account and follow @nozbe, and then you'll be able to send direct messages from Twitter to your Nozbe inbox.

· **To add tasks to Nozbe inbox from your email**, click on "Your Nickname and PIN" tab, type in a nickname and a numerical PIN code. Now, Nozbe will generate the email address nickname.pin@nozbe.me that you'll use to post tasks from your email directly to your Nozbe inbox. As an example here, the nickname is "Chris" and the PIN is "213982," and so the generated email address will be chris.213982@nozbe.me. So, when I want to forward tasks to Nozbe inbox from my email, I compose an email message to chris.213982@nozbe.me, as shown in the screenshot below.

The 4 Hour Work Week Tool Box

As you can see in the screenshot above, I'm sending several tasks to the Nozbe inbox and putting a dot before each task's name so that Nozbe can delineate between each task to be added. Furthermore, if I need to add some details to a task, I can simply type in a text comment in the next line to the task name. In this example, I added a comment to the first task, and now let's see what this email translates into in my Nozbe inbox.

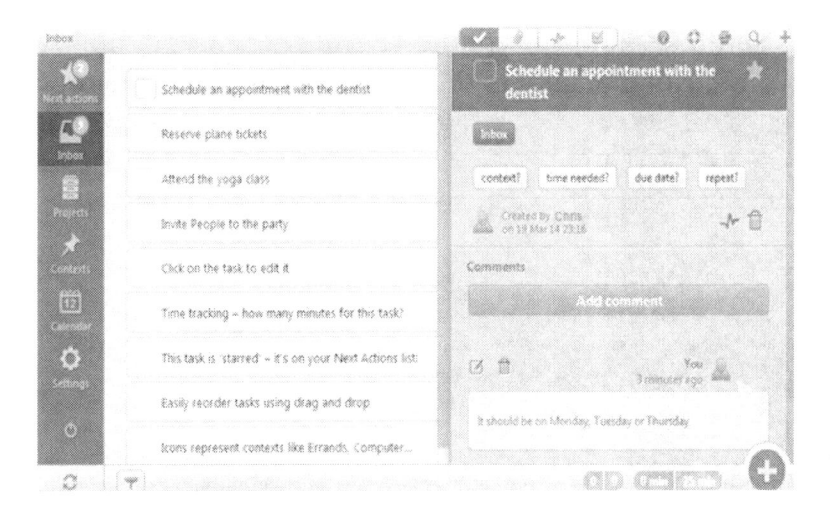

As you can see in the above screenshot, the three tasks in the email are now added at the top of Nozbe inbox, and the comment in the first task is added in its comments section. Pretty slick!

The Top Toolbar

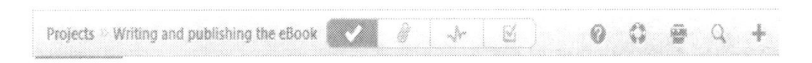

The above screenshot shows the toolbar at the top of Nozbe screen. Beginning from the left hand side:

115

The 4 Hour Work Week Tool Box

·   **A display of the current place you're viewing**. Here, it's "Projects," and the name of the project being viewed.

·   **The check mark** shows the active tasks.

·   **The paperclip symbol** shows you the attachments you provided for the current project. In Nozbe, you can add text notes, Evernote notes, and attach files from your computer and from your Dropbox account. Notable here is that the attachments and notes that are added are actually potential tasks, as you're allowed to create a new task with every attachment or note you add, as you can see in the screenshot below.

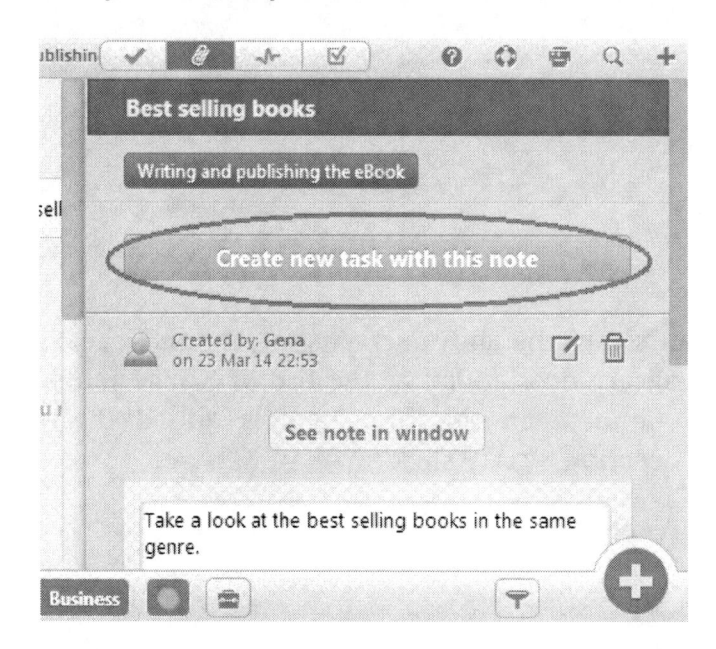

Back to functions in the screen top toolbar:

The 4 Hour Work Week Tool Box

- **The pulse symbol** shows you all your activities in the current project.

- **The paper with the check mark** shows the completed tasks.

The remaining features are:

- The tutorial video that guides you through using the basic features of Nozbe

- The contact form where you can contact Nozbe team and send them your feedback and any questions you might have

- Print the current view

- Search

- And the plus sign that allows you to add tasks to any location in your Nozbe account.

Having reviewed the basic features of Nozbe, let's now take a look at the pricing plans.

Pricing plans

The free plan allows up to 5 incomplete projects/contexts. If you need to have more than 5 contexts and/or more than 5 incomplete projects at a time, then you need to upgrade to one of the paid plans.

For each paid plan, you can choose to pay monthly or annually. If you choose to pay monthly you'll pay the full price, but if you choose to pay annually you'll save 20%

The 4 Hour Work Week Tool Box

of the price. In addition, Nozbe provides 60-day money-back guarantee. Paid plans are as follows:

- **Personal:** single user, $8 per month, $96 billed annually ($10 per month if paid monthly). If you have a free account, you can go to your account settings and upgrade to this plan and enjoy a 30-day free trial period.

- **Family:** up to 5 users, $16 per month, $192 billed annually ($20 per month if paid monthly)

- **Team:** up to 20 users, $40 per month, $480 billed annually ($50 per month if paid monthly)

Nozbe for mobile

In addition to their web app that works with any browser, Nozbe provides apps for Macs, iPhones, iPads, Android phones and tablets, in addition to the upcoming Windows Phone app and Blackberry app, which are expected to be available by late 2014.

Earn Money Promoting Nozbe

You can recommend Nozbe to other people and get a commission for every person who signs up with the service. The commission is recurring and applies to all Nozbe plans; if the new customer creates a free account, you'll earn a 10% lifetime commission, and if you refer someone and he creates a paid account, you'll earn a 20% lifetime commission from every payment they make. When your commissions reach or exceed $100, Nozbe will pay you the money plus 20% payout bonus. To earn money with Nozbe, open "Settings" and scroll down to

The 4 Hour Work Week Tool Box

"How to recommend Nozbe and earn money." Under that title you'll find your unique Nozbe affiliate link that you can use to recommend Nozbe to other people.

Here's the bottom line with Nozbe: Its every bit as good as my personal favorite Trello. I think that Trello does have more features in its free version, but I think its worth trying out both of these platforms (and Asana, which I'll talk about below) and decide what works best for *you*. Like any productivity tool, you don't want the fanciest or trendiest tool—you want the one that you're going to actually use!

Chapter Three: Asana

Asana is another highly featured task management app and a popular choice for effectively managing projects. With its powerful capabilities, Asana has a really robust selection for managing tasks and projects of all types and sizes.

What makes Asana different from both Trello and Nozbe is that it is mainly designed for managing teamwork tasks/projects, and at the same time it provides a private space for each member of the working team to manage their personal tasks/projects.

To start using Asana, go to www.asana.com and sign up for a free account. Similar to Trello, you can either go through the traditional sign up process and type in an email and a password, or sign up with your Google account which is strongly recommended for the same reason as in Trello: the ability to attach items directly from your Google Drive to Asana Tasks.

The unique thing about creating an account on Asana is that you have to create a workspace in order for the account to be created. The workspace that you'll create is associated with a team that consists of up to fifteen members. What this means is that you have to invite at least one person to create a team for your first workspace and then you'll be able to launch your account.

What actually happens when you sign up with Asana is that the app prompts you to enter the name of your first workspace, the name of the team associated with that workspace, and the names and email addresses of the persons that will become members of that team. Afterwards, Asana will email these persons with an invitation to create an account on Asana and join your team for your first workspace.

Having launched your account on Asana, you can create as many workspaces as you want, and for every workspace, you can invite up to 15 persons to join the associated team. You can also use the "Personal Projects" workspace, which is an individual workspace that Asana provides for you so that you can use it to manage the tasks and projects that you want to handle without a team.

Having explained how to create an account on Asana, I'll now walk you through all the basic features in the app, and explain how to use them to establish and use a successful task management system.

The task management structure

Asana provides a thoroughly organized task management structure that consists of the following elements:

Workspace → Project → Section (optional) → Task → Subtask (optional)

"Section" and "Subtask" are optional elements in that you have a choice as to whether or not to add "Sections" within any given Project and/or add 'Subtasks" within any given Task. The screenshot below shows you a typical example on how this structure can be set up. This

The 4 Hour Work Week Tool Box

screenshot is going to be your reference as we go through the details of how to set up and use the task management structure in Asana.

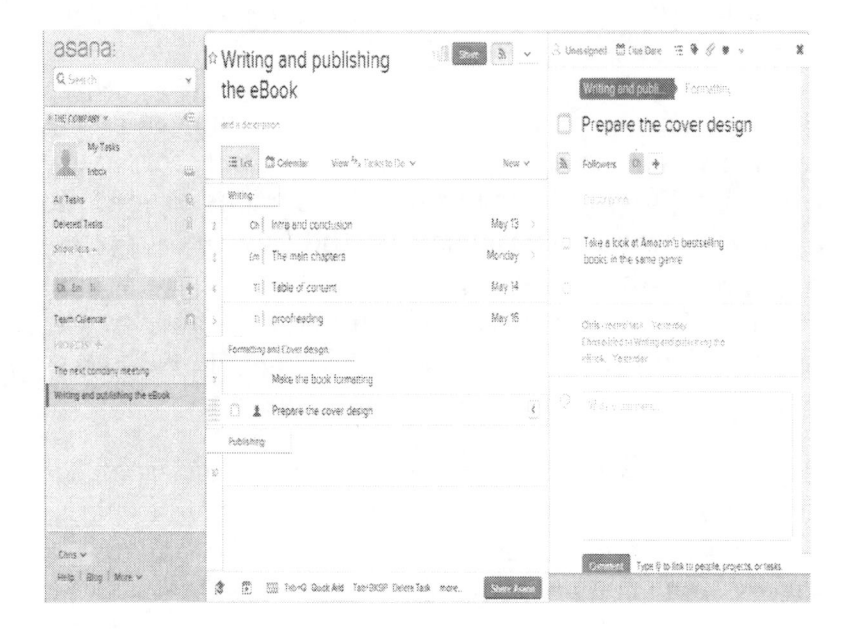

As you see in the above screenshot, the screen consists of three panes:

•   **The left pane** includes account settings, team members of the current Workspace, and the names of the Projects within the current Workspace.

•   **The center pane** shows the tasks and sections within the current Project.

•   **The right pane**, which is called the Task pane, includes all the items and activities within the current Task.

The 4 Hour Work Week Tool Box

The Project

The screenshot below depicts the left pane of the screen. The lower part of the screenshot is "Projects," which shows you all the Projects within the current Workspace. The button with the plus sign that you see beside "Projects" is what you click to create a new Project.

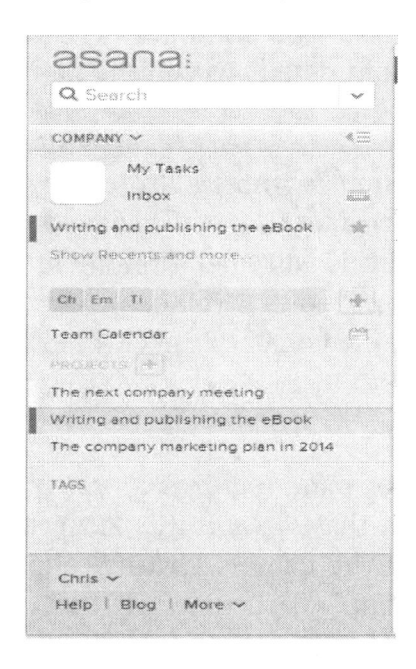

When you create a new Project, as you can see in the screenshot below, you'll be prompted to enter a name for this Project on top of the center pane, and then you can create Tasks within that new project.

The 4 Hour Work Week Tool Box

When you click on "Add a Task," you'll be prompted to enter a name for the new Task. Now the right pane (Task pane) will be open for you to add details within the new Task.

You can also create a new item within a Project by clicking on "New" - the down arrow at the right hand side of the above screenshot - and this will open up a menu that includes "Task" and "Section," so that you can create a Task or add a Section within the current Project.

Managing Projects

In the screen below, the center pane features a typical Project. The Project name is at the top, and this Project includes two Sections holding the names "Writing" and "Formatting and Cover Design." Each one of these Sections includes a number of Tasks.

The 4 Hour Work Week Tool Box

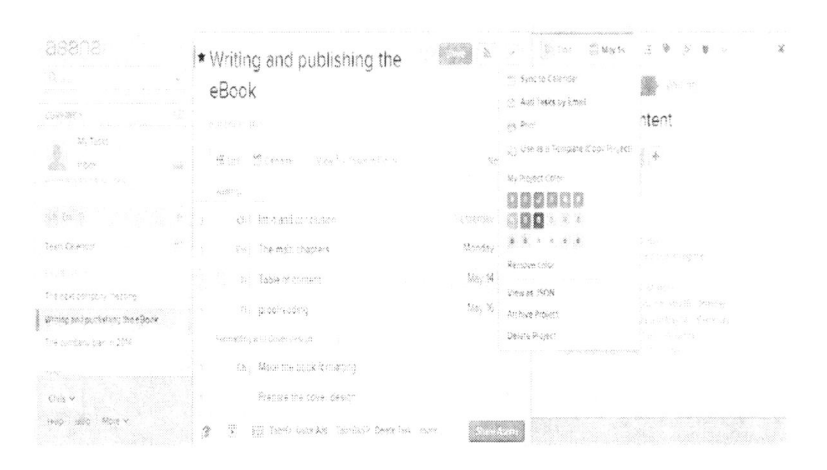

In addition to the components of the Project, the center pane also includes the following features and actions:

Clicking on the star next to the Project name adds this project to your "Favorites" section that lies in the left pane right under the inbox

The "Share" button opens up a window where you can choose whether to make the Project private or public. Also, for public Projects, this window includes a search field where you can type in the names and emails of the people with whom you want to share the Project.

The button with the RSS sign allows you to follow the current Project in order to get a notification message in your Asana Inbox of every new activity a team member does in the Project.

Clicking on the dropdown arrow next to the RSS button opens up a menu that includes "Print" and "Delete Project" and the following functions:

The 4 Hour Work Week Tool Box

Sync to Calendar: This gives you a link that you can use to sync the due dates of the incomplete Tasks in Asana to the calendar app that you're usually using. What you do to make that sync is that you take that link and put it into your calendar app (shortly, I'll explain how to do this), and then you'll be able to access the incomplete Tasks in Asana from your calendar app. Asana syncs your tasks with the following calendar apps:

• *Google Calendar:* Go to your Google Calendar, open the "Other calendars" dropdown menu that you see in the screenshot below, select "Add by URL," and enter the link that Asana provides for syncing with Google Calendar.

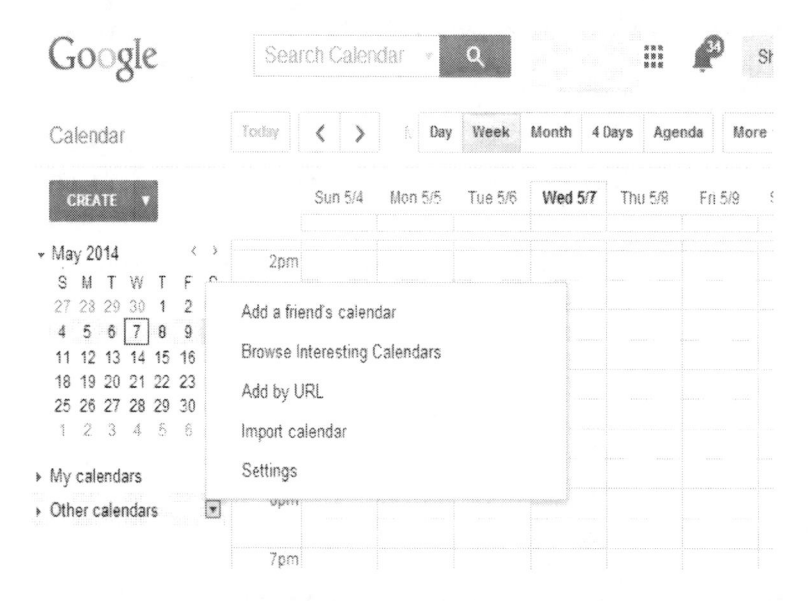

• *ICAL, Outlook, or other calendars:* Asana provides a URL that, when clicked, opens up your default calendar app.

126

The 4 Hour Work Week Tool Box

Add Tasks by Email: Asana allows both adding individual tasks via email, and emailing tasks to existing projects. Later in this chapter you'll see a detailed explanation on how to use email to create tasks, and what the details of the sent email translate into.

Use as a Template: This keeps a copy of the current Project for you to use as a template to create similar projects. The same function can be initiated by opening the dropdown menu that appears when you hover with your mouse cursor on a Project in the left pane and choosing "Use as a Template" that you see in the below screenshot. This feature is extremely useful if you have some projects that you do regularly and you follow the same steps every time you launch these projects. Interview questions, new hire onboarding, new client checklists, and press launches are typical examples of the projects that can be used as templates. For example, you can create a Project on Asana for the new hire onboarding, and then use that Project as a template that you can use to directly create similar new hire onboarding projects in the future.

The 4 Hour Work Week Tool Box

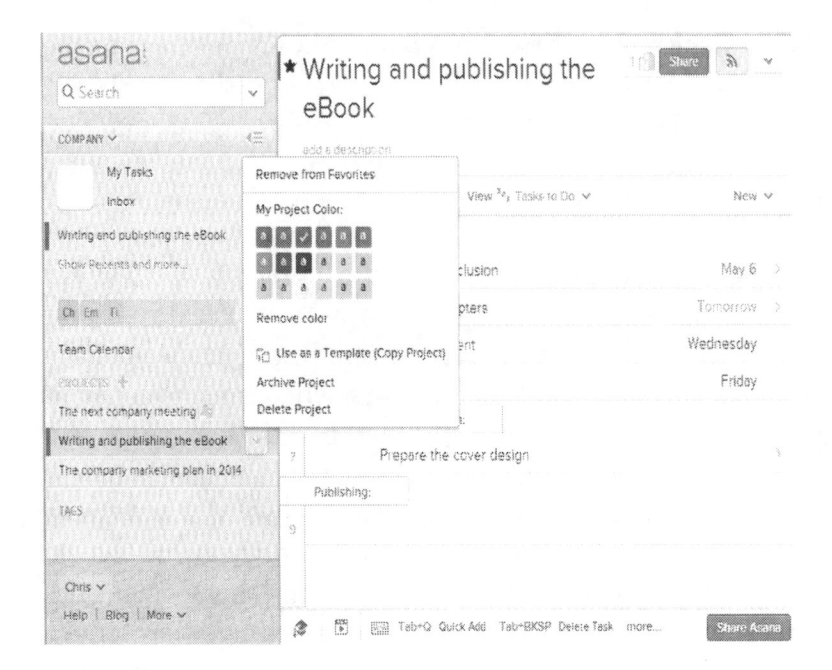

My Project Color allows you to color-code the current Project.

View as JSON opens the current Project in the JavaScript Object Notation form.

Working Within a Project in Asana

In the center pane, as you see in the screenshot below, there are three items that appear when you hover with your mouse cursor on a Task name: a head, a grid, and a checkbox.

128

The 4 Hour Work Week Tool Box

Clicking on the head symbol opens up a field where you can type in the name or email address of the person to whom you want to assign the task.

Holding down the left click on the grid symbol allows you to change the Task's position within the Project by dragging and dropping.

The checkbox is what you click when the Task is completed and if you click on the arrow next to the Task name, you'll open up the Task status window in the right pane (depicted below).

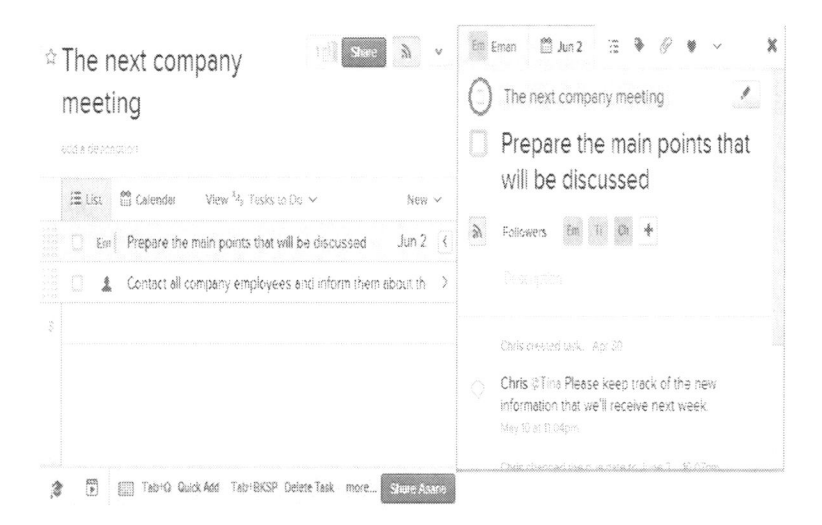

Managing Tasks

As depicted in the screenshot above, from the top of the right pane all the way down to the bottom, the following details represent the Task status:

129

The 4 Hour Work Week Tool Box

·   The top toolbar includes the Task functions that will be explained below.

·   The name of the current Project – in this example, it's "The next company meeting" – and if you hover on it with your mouse cursor, a clipboard sign will show up; it's the sign that you see in the above screenshot that's circled in red. Clicking on that clipboard sign allows you to change the location of the current Task; you can put it under another Project, or create a new Project and put this Task in it.

·   The name of the current Task.

·   The Followers of the Task. These people receive notifications in both email and their Asana Inbox about all the activities that happen within the Task.

·   The Task description.

·   The commenting area where team members can share their thoughts on the Task.

The top toolbar in the right pane includes the following functions:

Clicking on the first button from the left hand side opens up a window that features all the team members of the current Workspace. From that window, you can select the assignee of the current Task.

Clicking on the next button opens up a window that features a calendar so that you can set a due date for the current Task. That window also includes a "Set to repeat"

130

The 4 Hour Work Week Tool Box

button that allows you to specify the repeating interval, if you want the current Task to be repeated.

The button with the list symbol allows you to add subtasks within the current Task.

The button with the tag symbol allows you to add a tag to the Task. That tag can be used to create filtered views of Tasks across Projects.

The paperclip button allows you to attach files to the Task. You can attach files from your computer, Dropbox, and Google Drive.

The down arrow at the end of the toolbar opens up a menu that includes "Delete Task," "Print, " and the following actions:

Make a Copy allows you to use the current Task as a template, and then it allows you to name the new Task and choose the elements of the original Task that you need to keep in the new Task. You can choose to keep "Task Description," "Assignee," "Subtasks," "Attachments," "Tags," "Followers," and/or "Due Date" of the original Task, and put them in the new Task.

Merge Duplicate Tasks closes the current Task, and adds its tags, a back-link to it, and its followers to another Task within the current Project. You can use this feature within any given project when you find that there are two Tasks that can be merged into one Task.

Adding tasks via email

The 4 Hour Work Week Tool Box

As you've seen earlier in this chapter, Asana allows creating tasks via email. In this regard, Asana allows both of following: creating individual tasks and creating tasks under existing projects.

Emailing individual tasks

x@mail.asana.com is the email address that you can use to send a task via email to any given Workspace, and the emailed task will appear in "My tasks" that you can see at the top of the left pane depicted in the first and second screenshots in this chapter. Here's those screenshots again for your reference:

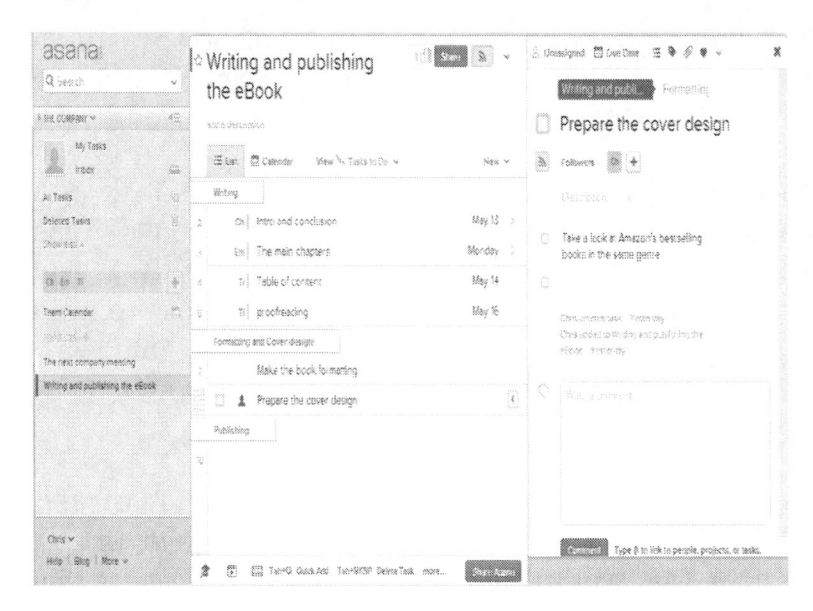

The 4 Hour Work Week Tool Box

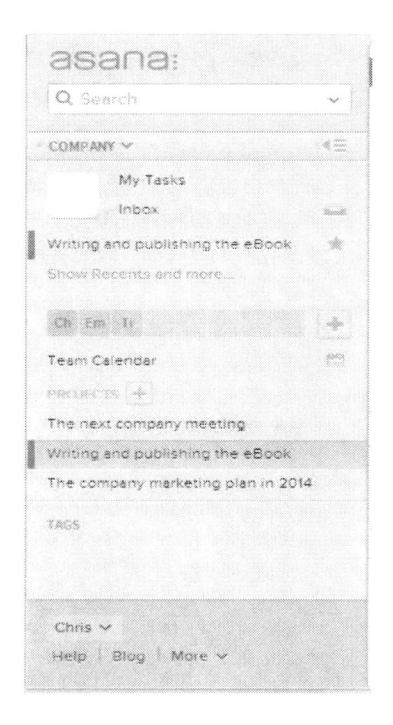

Here is what the emailed task translates into in the "My tasks" list:

· The subject of the email will be the task name

· The body of the email message will become the task description

· The email attachments will be attached to the task.

· People in the CC field will be the task followers.

Emailing tasks to existing projects

The following example is a step-by-step explanation on how to email a task to an existing project.

The 4 Hour Work Week Tool Box

First, find the project ID: For any given project, when you click on the project name in the left pane or in the center pane, or when you click on a task within that project, the URL for the webpage becomes https://app.asana.com/0/FirstNumber/SecondNumber. That "FirstNumber" in the URL is actually the project ID.

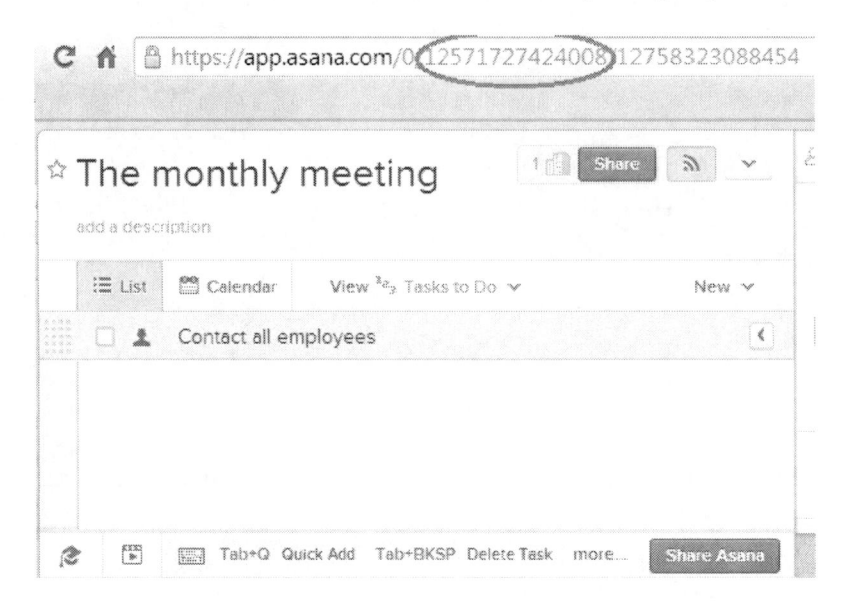

As an example, the screenshot above depicts a typical project named "The monthly meeting," and the project ID, as it appears inside the red oval shape, is 12571727424008.

Second, email a task to the project: For this purpose, you'll use the email address x+FirstNumber@mail.asana.com. In our example, the email address will be x+1257172742488@mail.asana.com. The screenshot below depicts a typical task being emailed to "The monthly meeting" project.

134

The 4 Hour Work Week Tool Box

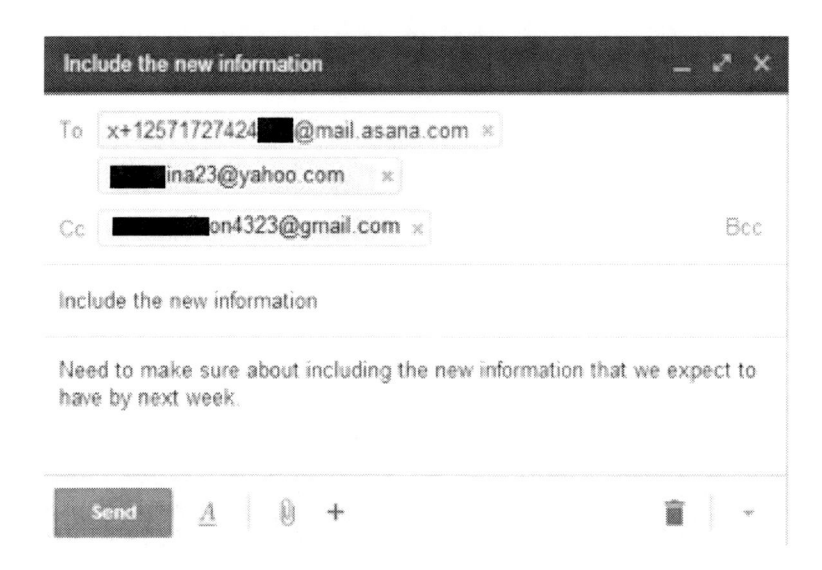

Include the new information

To: x+12571727424█@mail.asana.com ×
   █ina23@yahoo.com ×
Cc: █on4323@gmail.com ×   Bcc

Include the new information

Need to make sure about including the new information that we expect to have by next week.

Send

Here is what the email above translates into:

- The email subject will be the task name.

- The email body will be the description of the task.

- The person(s) in the CC field will be the task follower(s).

- The person sharing the "To:" field with the email address will be the Assignee of the task.

- If the email has attachments, the attached items will be added as attachments to the new task.

The screenshot below depicts the task after it has been emailed.

The 4 Hour Work Week Tool Box

As you see above, the emailed task is named "Include the new information," and it now appears in the center pane within "The monthly meeting" project. The right pane features the details of that emailed task: the task name, description, followers, and the assignee.

Views

There are a number of filtered views that allow you, within a specific Project, to see only the Tasks that meet specific criteria. Asana provides the following Task views: "List," "Calendar," and "View 123 Tasks to Do" which is the default view that you see when you open Asana. It includes all the Tasks that you're assigned to, along with all the Tasks that you're following. The screenshot below depicts the center pane, and you can see all the available Task views listed in a dropdown menu that appears when you click on the "View" button.

The 4 Hour Work Week Tool Box

As you can see in the above screenshot, clicking on the "View" button opens up a menu that includes the following Task filtering criteria:

· **Recently Completed Tasks** shows only the tasks that have been completed recently.

· **All Tasks** shows both completed and incomplete Tasks.

· **Tasks by Due Date** orders Tasks that have due dates from the nearest date to the latest date.

· **Tasks by Assignee** lists the Tasks that are assigned to every member of the working team.

In addition, the above list includes "Save as Default View for Everyone," which allows you to choose any one of the listed views and set it to be the default view for all the team members.

The 4 Hour Work Week Tool Box

Subtasks

As you have seen earlier in this chapter, you can create Subtasks within any given Task in Asana. The screenshot below depicts a typical Task featured in the right pane of Asana screen. Depicted also is the top toolbar that includes a button that has a list symbol on it. Clicking on that a button adds a Subtask under the current Task. You can see the added Subtask showing up at the bottom of the screenshot.

As you see in the screenshot, when you hover your mouse cursor on the Subtask, these Subtask functions will show up:

On the left hand side of the Subtask name:

•   The grid symbol allows you to change the location of the Subtask by dragging and dropping.

•   The checkbox that you click when the Subtask is completed.

On the right hand side of the Subtask name:

The 4 Hour Work Week Tool Box

· <u>The calendar symbol</u> allows you to add a due date for the Subtask.

· <u>The head symbol</u> allows you to send an email invitation to the person to whom you want to assign the Subtask.

· <u>The comment symbol</u> is where you can communicate with your teammates and convey your thoughts about the Subtask.

The Left Pane

The screenshot below depicts the left pane of Asana screen.

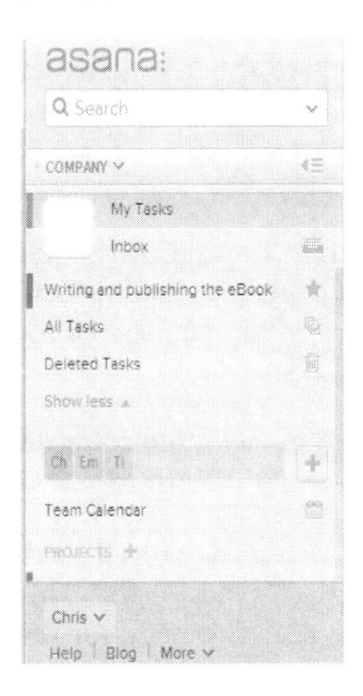

The 4 Hour Work Week Tool Box

As you see in the above screenshot, besides the team members and the Projects within the current Workspace, the left pane includes these features: My Tasks, Inbox, Search, Account Settings, Workspace Settings, and the Team Calendar.

My Tasks

Within any given workspace, "My tasks" is the place where you see all the tasks that you're contributing to as an assignee or as a follower. Also, as explained earlier in this chapter, it's the default destination of the emailed tasks.

Inbox

It's where you receive notifications of the new activities your team members do in the tasks that you're following.

Search

As you see in the above screenshot, the top of the left pane features a search field that you can use to find items within the current Workspace. You can search for items by either of the following ways:

- **Type in an item's name**: This will allow you to search for people, Projects, Tasks, Subtasks, or tags.

- **Click on the down arrow within the search field**: This will open up a window named "Find Tasks." This window allows you to specify the search criteria for the Task(s) that you want to find. The search criteria includes "Contains the words," "Assigned to," "In projects," "Tagged with," the due date, whether or not the task has attachments, and whether the task is completed or incomplete. In addition, clicking on "Search by Another Field" that you see in the screenshot below opens up a list that includes a host of other search criteria that you can use to search for Tasks.

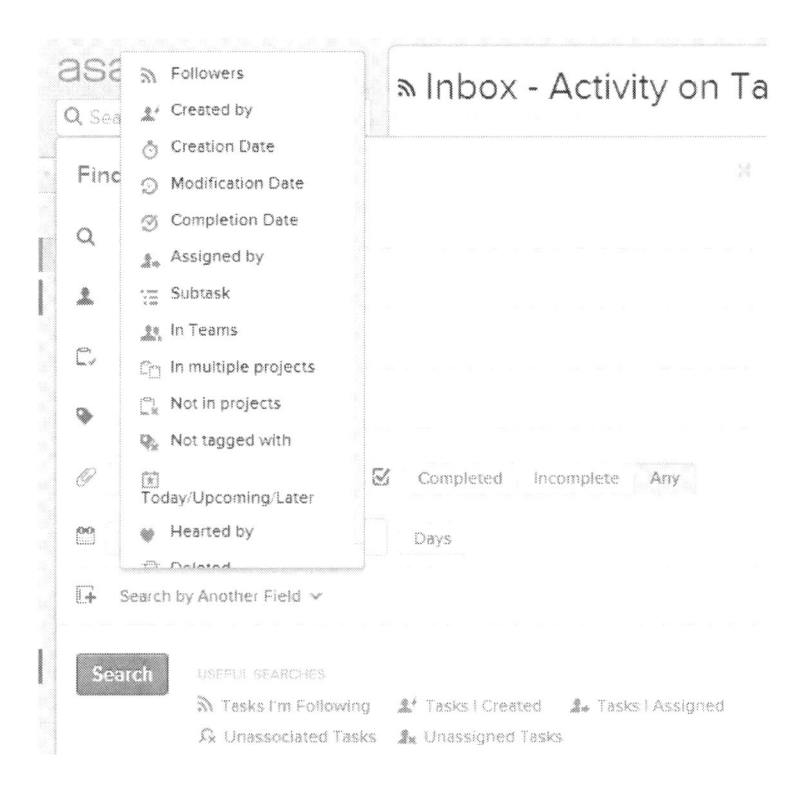

Account Settings

The screenshot below depicts the bottom part of the left pane.

The 4 Hour Work Week Tool Box

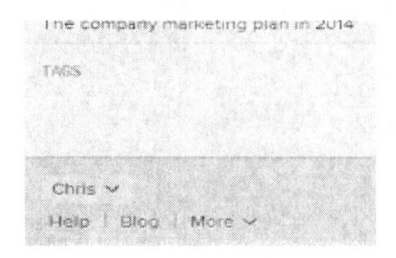

Clicking on the button depicted above that has the name of the account owner – "Chris" in this example – opens up a list that includes two items: "Account Settings" and "New Workspace." In Asana, you can create as many Workspaces as you want. When you click on "New Workspace," you'll be prompted to type in the name of the new Workspace that you'll create, along with the email addresses for the persons who you want to join your new Workspace.

Account settings

Account settings include the following features:

• <u>Profile</u> is where you edit your name and/or change your avatar.

• <u>To Email</u> is where you set the email addresses where you want Asana email notifications to be sent.

• <u>From email</u> is where you set the email address that you'll use to send Tasks to a certain Workspace. If you have more than one Workspace, you'll set one email address for each Workspace.

• <u>Account</u> is where you change your password if you need to.

The 4 Hour Work Week Tool Box

- <u>Apps</u> is where you connect Asana with your favorite apps. For this purpose, Asana provides an API key that you can use to integrate Asana with external apps.

- <u>Hacks</u> include some experimental features developed by Asana's team. They made these features available so that you can use them to enhance the performance of your account. These experimental features include:

- ***Inbox Counter*** shows you the number of new notifications that you've received since you last checked your Inbox.

- ***Inbox Snooze*** hides all incoming messages to your Inbox for one hour. This feature could be helpful if you need some time to focus on your work and you don't want to be distracted by a new messages coming to your Inbox.

- ***Add up Numbers in Brackets*** is a useful feature for doing tasks that include adding up costs. After activating this feature, and when you select several tasks that start with a number in brackets, then the right pane will show you the sum.

Workspace Settings

The screenshot below depicts the top section of the left pane.

The 4 Hour Work Week Tool Box

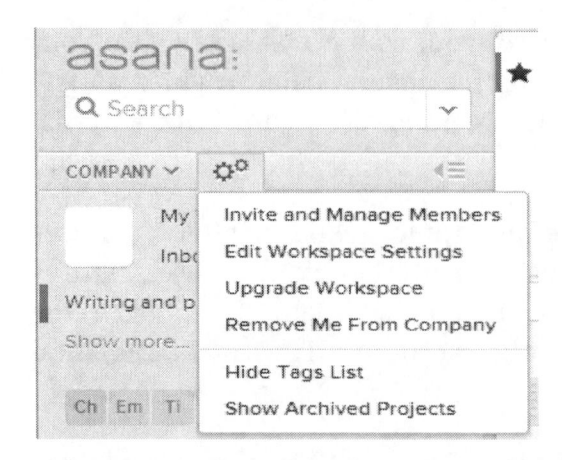

Clicking on the button above that has the current Workspace name on it ("Company" in this example) opens up a list of all the Workspaces that you have, including the "Personal Projects" Workspace that Asana provides by default.

Also, if you hover with your cursor on the button that has the Workspace name on it, a double-gear button will show up that, when clicked, opens up the workspace settings menu, shown above.

Besides "Show Archived Projects," the workspace settings menu includes the following functions:

· **Invite and manage members** opens up the "Manage Workspace" window below.

The 4 Hour Work Week Tool Box

> **Manage Workspace: Company**
>
> SETTINGS | **MEMBERS** | ADVANCED
>
> 3 MEMBERS (of 15 available) Upgrade to Get More Members »
>
> Chris
>
> Eman
>
> Tina
>
> ADD MEMBERS TO COMPANY
> Email | Name (optional)
> [   ]   Send Invite
>
> ☐ Guest

As you see in the screenshot above, the top of "Manage Workspace" window features three tabs: "Settings," "Members," and "Advanced."

- Settings allows you to edit the name of the Workspace, and specify what this Workspace is intended for: "Business," "Nonprofit," "School," "Household," "Club/Team," or "Other."

- Members is where you send email invitations to the people you want to join your team for the current Workspace (again, your team can have up to 15 members). If you want to add a specific person to your team and you want him to have a restricted access to the Workspace, click inside the "Guest" checkbox that you see at the bottom of the above screenshot. Adding a person as a guest allows them to only see the projects and tasks that are shared directly with them.

The 4 Hour Work Week Tool Box

·   <u>Advanced</u> allows you to activate the "Harvest" time-tracking app. Activating Harvest will add a time tracking button to the toolbar at the top of the right pane.

·   **Upgrade Workspace** allows you to upgrade your account to one of the Asana paid plans that will be discussed later in this chapter.

·   **Remove me from [the Workspace name]** removes you from the current Workspace, and then you'll not be able to access any of the Projects or Tasks within it. If you want to join that Workspace again, you'll need to ask one of its team members to invite you to join the Workspace.

Team Calendar

If you go back to the screenshot that depicts the left pane, you'll see the "Team Calendar" feature that allows you to have a calendar view of all the Tasks within the current Workspace. The screenshot below depicts what you see when you click on "Team Calendar."

The 4 Hour Work Week Tool Box

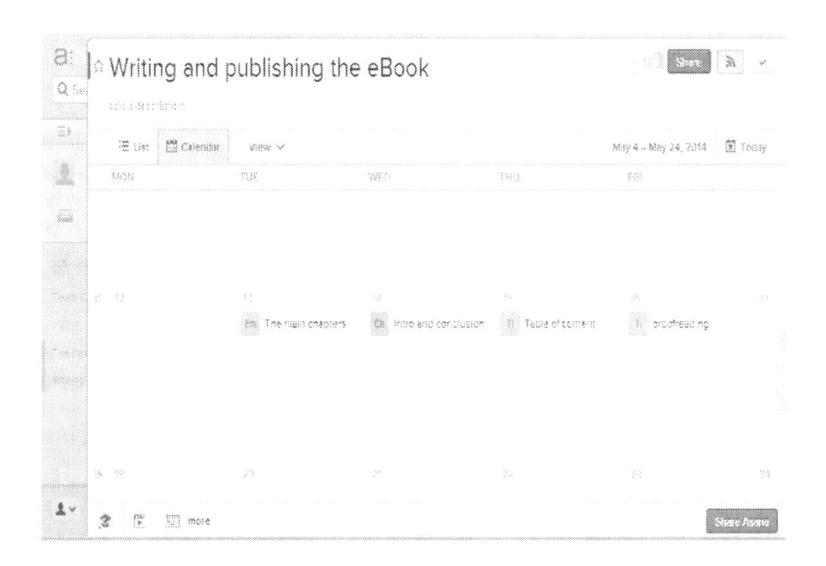

As you see in the screenshot above, every Task shows up on the calendar day that represents its due date, and you can also see the avatars of the team members to which the tasks are assigned. Beside the "Team Calendar," there is another way to invoke the calendar view of the tasks, and that's by clicking "All Tasks" in the left pane, and then clicking on the "Calendar" view in the center pane.

The cool thing about the "Team Calendar" feature is that it's an intuitive way that allows every team member to visualize how the whole team is moving forward. Moreover, when you're on the "Team Calendar" view, you can simply change the due date for any Task by dragging and dropping. And if you click on any Task, this will open up a fully-featured task management window where you can edit the Task name, change the assignee, add Subtasks, put on a label, attach files from your computer, Dropbox, Google Drive, change the Task location, add followers, and/or add comments. In addition, you can

The 4 Hour Work Week Tool Box

delete the task, use it as a template, and/or merge it with another Task.

The Bottom Toolbar

The screenshot below depicts the toolbar that you can see at the bottom of the center pane.

As you see in the above screenshot, the bottom toolbar includes the following features:

·   **The graduation cap symbol** is the getting-started guide that takes you through how to use Asana.

·   **Clicking on the video player symbol** opens up a list of videos that show various tips and tricks on how to get things done with Asana.

·   **The keyboard symbol (the same as "more")** opens up a list of keyboard shortcuts for some features in Asana.

·   **Quick Add** allows you to add tasks to the current workspace. Clicking on "Quick Add" opens up a window where you put a name and description for the new task, assign the task to a team mate, add to a project, add tags, due date, attach a file, and/or add followers.

·   **Clicking on "Tab+BKSP" or "Delete Task"** deletes the current item.

The 4 Hour Work Week Tool Box

- **Share Asana** allows you to invite people to use Asana by tweeting about it and/or giving it a "Like" and "Share" on Facebook.

The Premium Workspace

Besides the highly useful free plan, Asana provides a Premium Workspace that is available at $50 per month. Upgrading the free account to the Premium Workspace allows you to enjoy the following enhanced features. For what its worth, I don't think that the Premium membership is worth it for Asana, as the basic free program has a ton of useful features and you don't get that much more in the Premium version.

- **Project-level permissions:** You'll be allowed to share private projects with a small group within a particular workspace.

- **Priority support:** You'll get a greater access to support.

- **Automatic upgrades:** When new features are added to Asana, your account will be upgraded for no extra fee.

- **Add more than 15 members** which is available according to the following plans:

- $100 per month allows you to make a team of up to 30 members.

- $300 per month allows you to make a team of up to 50 members.

The 4 Hour Work Week Tool Box

- $550 per month allows you to make a team of up to 75 members.

- $800 per month allows you to make a team of up to 100 members.

Asana for Mobile

Besides the web app, Asana provides native apps for both iPhone and Android devices. The iPhone app is available in the App Store, and the Android app is available in Google Play Store. You can also access Asana mobile app from Android and iOS smartphones by visiting app.asana.com from your mobile browser. For the iPad, you can access Asana by visiting the Asana mobile site on Safari.

Asana mobile apps are highly featured tools that allow you to efficiently manage your Asana account. By using Asana mobile apps, you can do the following actions:

- Browse your inbox.

- Search for tasks.

- Reorder tasks by dragging and dropping.

- Add and edit tasks and sections.

- Add and edit due dates, descriptions, followers, and projects of any task.

- Create new projects for existing tasks.

- Attach files to tasks.

The 4 Hour Work Week Tool Box

In summary, Asana is a great project management tool, and as I've previously said, I believe that trying each of these programs—made easier because they're free—and seeing what works for you is the best way to judge what the right platform is for YOU. Having said that, let's compare all three programs head-to-head.

The 4 Hour Work Week Tool Box

Chapter Four: Comparison and Bottom Line

Now, and after reviewing three of the most popular task management platforms, Trello, Nozbe, and Asana, let's see how they compare to each other in terms of all the elements that matter to us as end users.

Orientation: Both Trello and Nozbe are basically oriented towards the individual user, and so the user can launch an account, and then they can build up their team by inviting people and assigning them to tasks. But in Asana, the teamwork-oriented platform, creating an account requires a team of at least two members. Personally, I think that the Asana requirement of having two people sign up to activate your account is a negative aspect of their program, so Trello and Nozbe get one point, Asana negative one point.

Sign up with Google: While Nozbe doesn't allow signing up with Google, both Trello and Asana allow you to sign up with your Google account. This feature allows you to attach items directly from your Google Drive to your Trello cards or Asana tasks. One point each for Trello and Asana, none for Nozbe.

The terminology: Basically, Trello, Nozbe, and Asana use nearly the same task management outlines but with different terminology, so one point to each program as each of these terminologies are easy to understand and use:

The 4 Hour Work Week Tool Box

- The "Organization" in Trello is the "Label" in Nozbe, and it is equivalent to the "Workspace" in Asana.

- The "Board" in Trello is the "Project" in both Nozbe and Asana.

- The "Card" in Trello is the "Task" in both Nozbe and Asana.

The hierarchy of task management structure:

Trello: Organization (optional) → Board → List → Card (task)

Nozbe: Label (optional) → Project → Task

Asana: Workspace → Project → Section (optional) → Task → Subtask (optional)

Asana enhances the task management structure with the two additional optional positions "Section" and "Subtask" that have no counterparts in both Trello and Nozbe. We'll give Asana another point for this.

The free account:

Trello: The free account provides unlimited open boards (projects), unlimited board members, and allows card (task) attachments of up to 10 MB size.

The 4 Hour Work Week Tool Box

Nozbe: The free account allows you to have 5 incomplete projects at a time, unlimited people in the project, and provides unlimited task attachment size.

Asana: The free account provides an unlimited number of workspaces and open projects, unlimited task attachment size, and allows each workspace team to include up to 15 members.

Points-wise, this is tough to declare a winner here. I think that Trello and Asana edge out Nozbe here, as the limitation of only 5 projects is somewhat of a limitation. So, I'll give one point each to Trello and Asana and none to Nozbe.

Creating individual tasks: This is where Trello falls short; the card (task) must come within a list within an existing board (project). On the other hand, both Nozbe and Asana allow you to create individual tasks that you can keep individual as they were created, put them under existing projects, or convert them into new projects. Sorry Trello, but Nozbe and Asana both win a point here.

Categorization: The three apps – Trello, Nozbe, and Asana – allow you to categorize the content of the task management platform you're using. However, each of the three platforms provides categorization of the content in a different concept from the other two platforms. Like the terminology, I think each program gets a point here as none of them are better or worse than the others:

Trello provides categorization of cards (tasks) into lists named "To Do," "Doing," and "Done" by default. However,

The 4 Hour Work Week Tool Box

you can manage these lists, rename, remove, and/or add as many lists as you need.

Nozbe provides categorization of projects and tasks into contexts. The context is the physical place (such as office, home, phone, etc.) where the project/task is supposed to be handled. For the free account, Nozbe provides five customizable contexts so that you can create the contexts that match your needs.

Asana provides categorization of workspaces. Categories of Workspaces are "Business," "Nonprofit," "School," "Household," "Club/Team," and "Other," in addition to the "Personal Projects" workspace which is dedicated to include all your personal-related projects.

Repeating (task) is available in both Nozbe and Asana, where you're allowed to schedule a task to reoccur every so often. Trello doesn't provide a similar feature, but I'm not taking a point off because in Trello you can copy checklists quite easily. One point to each program.

Paid plans:

Trello: Paid plans are based on the size of card (task) attachment.

Nozbe: Paid plans are based on the number of users for the account, and the number of projects/contexts within the account.

Asana: Paid plans are based on the number of team members per workspace. Paid plans also provide – within any give workspace – project-level permissions that allow you to share private projects with specific members of the team.

I think each program gets a point here, as each has some interesting features in the premium plans, but nothing Earth-shattering.

The Inbox:

Trello: No inbox

Nozbe: The inbox is the place where you can add standalone tasks.

Asana: The inbox is the place where you receive message notifications of new activities your team members do in the tasks that you're following.

In comparison to Nozbe, there are two features in Asana that are similar to Nozbe's inbox: "**Quick Add**" is the place where you can add standalone tasks, and **"My tasks"** list is the destination of the tasks created via email. Sorry Trello, but the lack of the inbox means one point each to Nozbe and Asana.

Building templates:

Trello provides building templates based on existing items; you can build board (project) templates, list templates, and card (task) templates.

Nozbe provides building project templates based on existing projects.

The 4 Hour Work Week Tool Box

Asana provides building both project templates and task templates. Moreover, you can either build templates based on existing items, or from scratch.

All three get a point here since you can template your work in each program.

Adding tasks via email:

Trello: For every board (project), Trello provides a unique email address that can be used to send cards (tasks) to that board.

Nozbe provides one email address that can be used to send individual tasks to the inbox.

Asana allows sending individual tasks, and also allows sending tasks to existing projects.

Once again, one point each for this nice feature.

Commenting and attachment options: the three platforms provide typing in text comments and URLs, and attaching files from Dropbox and from your computer. In addition, each one of the three platforms provides other options as follows:

In Trello, you can add checklists and attach files from Google Drive.

In Nozbe, you can add checklists and attach Evernote notes.

In Asana, you can add subtasks and attach files from Google Drive.

The 4 Hour Work Week Tool Box

Notice that Nozbe is the only platform here that has a connection with Evernote, and it's also the only platform that doesn't have a connection with Google Drive. Another thing is that while both Trello and Nozbe allow adding checklists to their tasks, Asana provides adding subtasks. Comparison wise, we can say that the subtask is an improved version of the checklist; while the checklist consists of a number of items, the subtask is like a checklist item that can have an assignee, due date, and comments. Bottom line: I'm not awarding any points here to any program, as I think that each program **should** have both Evernote and Google Drive integration.

Time elapsed between making an activity and seeing that activity done and getting an email notification in both Nozbe and Asana might extend to several minutes, while in Trello activities and email notifications appear in real time. This I find quite useful with Trello, so one point for Trello, none for the other two.

Archived items in both Trello and Asana remain available for viewing and/or restoring, but in Nozbe, archived items remain available for viewing and/or restoring only until the end of the day on which they were archived, and afterwards they become irretrievable. Huge problem with Nozbe here. I'm not awarding points to Trello and Asana, as this should be a basic, standard feature. I am, however, taking away a point from Nozbe.

Syncing tasks that have due dates to calendar apps: Asana allows you to sync the tasks that have due dates to your favorite calendar apps such as Google Calendar, ICAL, and Outlook. Nozbe and Trello don't provide a

The 4 Hour Work Week Tool Box

similar feature. One point to Asana, none to Nozbe or Trello.

Bottom Line

At the end of this book, and after reviewing the three task management apps, Trello, Nozbe, and Asana, and after we've seen how they compare to each other, now we come to the main question: which app is the best to use? Points-wise, here's where we ended up:

Trello: 10 points

Nozbe: 8 points

Asana: 11 points

The truth of the matter is that the answer to "which program to use" depends on several parameters specific to your needs. Your hoice depends on your style of managing your tasks/projects, the type and size of your tasks, the number of the projects that you need open at a time, and – if you're running teamwork projects – the number of your team members.

So, if you need a user-friendly tool that helps you organize all types of projects, Trello would probably be the best selection for you as long as the attachment to any given Trello card (task) doesn't exceed 10 MB size. If you're uploading a lot of video files, you're going to surpass 10 MB, but obviously for any other type of work, going above 10 MB would be rare.

If you need a flexible tool that allows you to create a task seamlessly whenever a new idea crosses your mind,

The 4 Hour Work Week Tool Box

Nozbe would be the best selection for you as long as you don't need to go beyond the five-open-projects threshold.

If you already have a team and you need a tool that allows you to organize your teamwork, and your personal/family related tasks as well, Asana will be the best selection for you.

And finally, whatever is the task management platform that you're going to use, it will a valuable addition to your lifestyle that will increase your efficiency and productivity, enhance the workflow of your business, and change your life for the better. Get started and try all three programs today and see what you like best!

The 4 Hour Work Week Tool Box

CONCLUSION

My sincere hope is not that you've enjoyed this book, but rather that you *take action*. Thoughts without action accomplish nothing, and only by employing the tactics and techniques in this book will you find any progress in your own life.

To that end, I'm always happy to connect with people and help them on their journey. Send me an email at contact@fourhourphysician.com and let me know your struggles, issues, and problem with your journey to achieve your own new-found, liberated life, and I'm glad to help you out!

Good luck!

The 4 Hour Work Week Tool Box

Disclaimer

All attempts have been made to verify the information contained in this book but the author and publisher do not bear any responsibility for errors or omissions. Any perceived negative connotation of any individual, group, or company is purely unintentional. Furthermore, this book is intended as a guide and as such, any and all responsibility for actions taken upon reading this book lies with the reader alone and not with the author or publisher. Additionally, it is the reader's responsibility alone and not the author's or publisher's to ensure that all applicable laws and regulations for business practice are adhered to. Lastly, I sometimes utilize affiliate links in the content of this book and as such, if you make a purchase through these links, I will gain a small commission. I have personally used each of the services listed in this book, however, and as such I can say that I would recommend them to my closest friend with the same ease that I now recommend them to you. My opinion is not for sale.

Copyright © 2014 by Creative Dynamics, LLC

All rights reserved. No part of this publication may be reproduced, distributed, or transmitted in any form or by any means, including photocopying, recording, or other electronic or mechanical methods, without the prior written permission of the publisher, except in the case of brief quotations embodied in critical reviews and certain other noncommercial uses permitted by copyright law.